Dear Susanna

Dear Susanna

It's Time for a Christian Renaissance

DAVID TORKINGTON

DARTON · LONGMAN + TODD

First published in 1999 by
Darton, Longman and Todd Ltd
1 Spencer Court
140–142 Wandsworth High Street
London SW18 4JJ

ISBN 0–232–52340–1

A catalogue record for this book is available
from the British Library.

Phototypeset by Intype London Ltd
Printed and bound in Great Britain by
Page Bros, Norwich, Norfolk

To Susanna
without whose inspiration
this book would never have been written

Contents

Introduction

Susanna was at primary school when I first met her. I came to know her and her family well until she went to university. Then we lost touch till I had a Christmas card from her about nine years ago to say she was married and living in London. She was pregnant with her first child, Michael, who was born the following February. Shortly afterwards her husband, Pat, was posted to Madrid where she had her second son, Matthew. After two years the family moved back to London where their third and fourth sons, Luke and Liam, were born. My wife and I were delighted when we were asked to be Liam's godparents.

Although we visited when we could we didn't write regularly until I received a letter from Susanna with a question that I tried to answer. She had given up a career as a teacher to become a full-time wife and mother and so felt somewhat put out by the traditional interpretation of the story of Martha and Mary. It gave an unwarranted explanation to the words of Jesus when he chided Martha for being 'busy about many things'.

Although she didn't present her reaction in so many words, it seems to me that Susanna had been made to feel like a second-class citizen in the Church where married life and motherhood came a poor second to a vocation to the religious life. The following series of letters grew out of her response to my letter, which inspired me to write many more. Some of them were published, with her permission, in the *Catholic Herald*, in the hope that they might be of help to others. I was surprised that so many found them helpful and as a result I decided to publish them in book form. However, I have added much new material to appeal to a wider readership – those who feel that the time is ripe for a genuine Christian Renaissance to prepare us to go forward in the Spirit of Christ into the third millennium.

1

The Siege Mentality

Dear Susanna,
You have asked enough difficult questions in the past, but this time you've surpassed yourself. How many priests and religious have left the Church since the Vatican Council? Why did they leave? Why couldn't they have stuck to their posts? Why have there been so many sexual scandals in recent years amongst the priests who remained behind? Whatever happened to the Vatican Council that seemed to promise so much? How can the Vision of Pope John be realised now when there seems to be such confusion everywhere? What can I do to help, as a married mother of four small boys?

Well, it will take much more than a single letter to try to answer all these questions; in fact it would take a whole book, but they're so important that I must do my best. The moment I heard you'd been asked to take a higher profile in the parish I knew you'd be bombarded with questions like these, not just from the mothers of the children you were teaching, but from your non-Catholic friends too. First of all let me say that no authentic renewal can begin without facing the truth, as fairly and squarely as possible, and that's no easy matter. The trouble is that those who should be spending their time preparing us for renewal have sadly been too busy trying to avoid the truth, covering it up instead of facing up to it, and I must take my share of the blame too.

In my years of writing as a Catholic journalist I haven't heard from anyone who seriously disagreed with me, at least about any major matter. However, far from making me feel smug, or deceiving myself into believing that everyone who reads my articles agrees with me, it gives me continual cause for concern.

You see, years ago I had a spiritual director who told me that if I were trying to speak the truth loud and clear I would inevitably suffer for it like so many others before me. When God used the Old Testament prophets to speak the truth to the people, many, if not the majority, hated the prophets for it because it threatened their vested interests, their privileged positions and their authority. It invariably shamed them too by highlighting their own moral depravity. Jeremiah is a case in point. He was vilified and almost put to death for daring to speak the truth. When he first heard that God wanted to make him a prophet he begged him to choose someone else, because he knew well enough what had happened to the prophets before him. He had no illusions about what happened to anyone who dared to speak the truth, and he was right.

The prophet Isaiah not only suffered as he did, but foretold that the greatest of all the prophets would suffer more than any other. Christ suffered that appalling and ignominious death on the cross because he dared to speak the truth to the very people who'd conveniently forgotten or trampled on it for the sake of the power and position that they coveted more than anything else. They might well have dressed as religious leaders and spoken in religious language like many of their contemporary counterparts, but that was just a front to enable them to maintain their lucrative jobs, their status and their positions of power over the people.

Now Christ made it clear that what happened to him would happen to those who wished to follow him. Not only would they antagonise the same authorities who crucified him and other authorities throughout the Roman Empire, but even their own families who would be divided by the truth that should have united them.

Time and time again those who have dared to speak the truth have had to suffer for it, as Christ did himself. For three centuries after the resurrection ordinary Christians suffered prolonged persecution and death for the faith that we can so easily take for granted. When St Athanasius came back from the Council of Nicaea he said that there was hardly a bishop there who had not been mutilated or tortured or who bore the marks of suffering of one sort or another.

A few weeks ago two Dominicans gave a seminar locally on their great preacher Savonarola, who was brutally tortured before being hanged and then publicly burnt for criticising not just the Medicis, but the clergy and the bishops too, and not least, the Pope himself! Now they are talking of canonising him with so many other great prophets, preachers and reformers, who were condemned in their lifetime by those who were busily employed in condemning or marginalising their spiritual successors – only to be canonised later, usually much later.

In our own time people like Martin Luther King, Steve Biko, Nelson Mandela, Alexander Solzhenitsyn and Oscar Romero are examples of what happens to those who are successful in speaking the truth to those who don't want to hear it.

Christ said that there would be two signs by which his disciples would be known: the first was the love that they would have for one another; the other was the way they would suffer for living and speaking the same truths that he died for.

I can't speak for you, but the older I get the more I feel I've shirked my responsibility to state the truth as clearly or as incisively as I should, come what may. Have I compromised my integrity because I want to maintain my position, my reputation, as a cosy, middle-of-the-road Catholic writer and journalist? Shouldn't I have spoken the truth more clearly, more openly, even if it cost me my job and my livelihood?

Why have so few people opposed or criticised me? Why have I not suffered as Christ did and other Christians throughout the ages? It's a question that I've been asking myself more urgently than ever since receiving your letter. My first reaction to your questions was to do, without thinking, what I've done so often in the past. Almost instinctively I begin to defend, to make excuses for the inexcusable. It's simply part and parcel of my Catholic upbringing. It's all part and parcel of my Catholic education too. You see, I grew up in an era when what was called the 'siege mentality' was the norm in the Catholic Church, when we still felt that our first responsibility as Catholics was to defend ourselves against a hostile world. This is why apologetics was such an important part of our education at school.

When I studied philosophy later on, much time was spent proving how other philosophic systems were wrong and how we were always right. It was the same in theology. All too much time was devoted to showing how heretics, and in particular the Protestant reformers, were wrong and how we were always right. Their views were invariably caricatured so at times I wondered how anyone could possibly hold them. They were set up like Aunt Sallies to be knocked to the ground by triumphant teachers, to the satisfaction of their students, including me! This created a certain smug arrogance that prevented us learning anything from outsiders, because we were always right. It also meant that the theology we learnt tended to concentrate on those truths that had been defined and underlined by the Church precisely because someone had denied or questioned them. Inevitably this meant that the presentation of the faith tended to be negative, lopsided and, frankly, rather boring. That is, of course, unless you got your kicks from seeing others, who couldn't defend themselves, knocked to the ground and booted about with impunity, because, as we were taught, 'error has no rights'!

It's the sort of theology that tends to appeal to ultra-conservatives, to right-wingers, to dogmatic authoritarians who like laying down the law to others and submitting themselves to legitimate authority, so long as it reinforces their particular prejudices. I have to say that it appealed to me too at the time, though I'm ashamed to admit it. That's why I know something about it.

Then quite out of the blue I had a sort of theological conversion experience when I was bowled over by what was called at the time the 'new theology' – but more of that later. The point I want to make for the present is that my conversion was predominantly intellectual and so despite the fact that my mind changed rather rapidly my emotions lagged behind. For very many years my instinctive reaction to any criticism of the Church I loved was to close ranks with others, even with those with whom I disagreed theologically, to defend it against all-comers. Even after very many years a carefully implanted bond of loyalty has led me to defend the indefensible. Only comparatively recently have I come to realise, not just with my head but with my heart too, that there is something more important than the Church on earth and that is the Kingdom of God. The Church is a means not an end. The time will come when the Church will come to an end, but God's Kingdom will go on for ever. The Church and everyone within it are called to perform a service for humanity and that is to bring on earth, as far as possible, the Kingdom of God or the rule of love that will one day reign for eternity. If there is something seriously wrong with the Church that prevents it from performing this function then it is wrong to pretend that all is well. Our first loyalty is to God and his Kingdom.

Human frailty, as history shows only too well, has diverted the Church from doing what Christ intended it to in the beginning. It has only been saved from disaster in the past thanks to the enduring promises of Christ and by the Holy Spirit speaking through men and women open enough to receive him. Endless cover-ups do the Church no good at all and a 'culture of cover-up' will prevent us seeing what needs to be changed. This means that the process of continual renewal, which is essential to the Church's well-being, will simply halt. Particularly since the Reformation, we have believed that our first duty is to defend and cover up anything that would give the impression to non-Catholics that anything could possibly be wrong with the Church. This 'culture of cover-up' that I have been a party to for all too long will continue until we all have the humility to accept that we have failed in so many ways, as Pope John Paul has stressed in his recent sermons. Only this humility will provide the means for God to give us the grace to see the source of our sickness and then the strength to do something about it.

I'll begin trying to answer your questions next time as honestly as my inhibitions will allow.

Love,
David

2

A Culture of Cover-up

Dear Susanna,
I suppose another reason why I haven't been as honest as I should in the past is because I've thought, 'Who am I to criticise other people's attitudes which were once my own?' Then when I reflected on the sort of people who have spoken out in the past and done so much for the Church by their honesty, they all seem to have been extraordinarily good people, if not saints. They were people with the sort of humility that allowed the Holy Spirit to enter into them, enabling them not just to see human failure and see it clearly, but to call people to change their lives, as they'd already changed theirs.

Frankly I just didn't see myself in that category, nor do I now for that matter. However I'm not setting myself up to judge others let alone to preach at them, but merely to start being a little more honest with myself and with others too – beginning with you. After all, the questions you've asked are on many people's minds and deserve the best and most honest answers that I can give: so here goes.

You may remember that I said that many of us in the Church, particularly of my generation, have been brought up in what I called the 'siege mentality'. Well, what I meant was that too much time and energy was spent desperately trying to cover up anything that could lead outsiders into believing that all was not well within the Church. For too long I've gone along with it, by managing to convince myself it was for the greater good.

Now don't get me wrong: I'm not saying that those who persist in doing this are bad men or bad women, because that is not necessarily the case. They have just been brought up, as I have, in 'a culture of cover-up' that has programmed them to cover up first and think later. They still think the Church's first job is to defend itself against a hostile world, and they do all they can to prevent that world from laying hands on ammunition to use against it. Truth is always the first casualty in war, and as long as the Church thinks it's at war with a hostile world then the truth will always suffer for the sake of expediency.

If the truth might be seen as giving rise to scandal then the truth must be sacrificed because there is nothing worse than scandal. Of course in such cases it's not the truth, but that's how it appears to people who are still suffering from the sort of 'pious paranoia' that once afflicted me. It prevents the Church from generating the kind of honesty and openness that is the indispensable prerequisite for authentic renewal. Whenever these Church defenders get a whiff of what could be serious scandal they follow their natural ecclesiastical instincts that tell them to keep quiet, let sleeping dogs lie as long as possible, in the hope that the problem will just go away, or that it will solve itself. And if, perish the thought, the press get hold of the story then they stand together and concoct the best damage-limitation exercise they can muster.

However, the real truth is that the Church is not living in a hostile world any longer. The world has what it believes to be far more important things to do than to attack the Church, which is for the most part seen as a total irrelevance anyway. Of course people love to hear and read about scandals, especially sexual scandals involving the clergy, but not because they feel threatened by the Church, but because they like to be entertained, and there's nothing funnier than seeing a person with pretensions, especially religious pretensions, slipping on a banana skin. The more pretentious the person the greater the amusement. If the Church wants to become relevant again it must start by both living and proclaiming the truth that is endlessly mocked by misuse.

If there's one thing that makes people sit up and listen it's sincerity, the truth. That's why everyone in the commercial or the political world who wants to be heard has to try to simulate sincerity and present their lies as truth. We have produced a generation of confidence tricksters who are all desperate to make a quick buck, or rise to positions of power by dressing up the truth in their own colours and making it dance to their tune. If the Church can only begin again by facing the truth of its own failure to live the gospel as it should, then that would be a beginning.

If the Church would only put aside all pretensions and the trappings of power and position and don sackcloth and ashes to repent of its complacency, then I believe that people would begin to listen, for only the humble can speak to the proud and hope to be heard.

All these matters are of such importance that I will return to them in my next letter.

Love,
David

3

More Prophets, Please

Dear Susanna,

I know that what I said in my last letter was pretty forthright, but I think the time for cover-up is at an end and it's time to start facing the truth as honestly as we can. You see all that I have experienced in the last fifty years or more has made me realise that the Church that we all love is in a serious state of spiritual decline. That's what Pope John had the honesty to see when few of his advisors could. This does not mean that the Church doesn't still proclaim the truth of the faith with certainty, nor does it mean that it does not stand for and proclaim important moral truths that are ignored in the contemporary moral morass that surrounds us. It has never done otherwise, but that is thanks to the promises of Christ and not to the unfortunate moral and spiritual behaviour of some who preach and proclaim the faith.

The message begins to sound hollow and meaningless when some of those who preach it suffer from an apparent spiritual emptiness that makes any thinking person realise that what has done nothing for the messenger can hardly be expected to do anything for the receiver. Yet we had the arrogance to dedicate the last decade of the second millennium to the task of evangelising the world, when it is we who must first be re-evangelised.

Humility is the indispensable ingredient for any authentic renewal. No, not renewal, that's an overworked word that has lost its meaning, and even at its best it tends to suggest something a little more superficial than the deep radical reform that is necessary. Humility means accepting the truth about oneself and about the Church to which we belong. Only those who can face the truth and speak the truth, whether it is welcome or unwelcome, can have any hope of reforming themselves and helping to take part in the reform of the Church.

The time for play-acting and pretence is over. The time for papering over the cracks is at an end. Now is the time for the truth, no matter how painful it may be. If we have failed – as we have – these failures must be seen and accepted openly, not endlessly covered up.

The spiritual disease that is undermining the body of Christ on earth cannot be arrested by pretending that it is not there. Nor can it be cured by using all sorts of phoney stratagems to hide its presence from those who suffer from it, and from those who might see it. I know many of these stratagems because I've used them often enough myself in the past! That the faithful must be protected from scandal at all costs is the usual excuse for covering up the truth, and so it goes on, so that the truth that would cry out for reform is never heard.

Another method used is to proclaim the importance of charity, insisting that we must never judge anyone and always put the best possible interpretation on the most reprehensible behaviour. This sort of attitude is not without merit in dealing with the minor faults and failings that flaw the best of us. However, when this approach is used to cover up repeatedly major forms of corruption then it makes a mockery of true charity. It is vital that corruption is exposed and removed before the damage is irreversible.

These are some of the subtle stratagems used by those who know that 'there but for the grace of discovery go I', or there, if the truth be discovered, goes the honour and reputation upon which our status and our positions of power and authority rest.

Every single reform that has been successful in the past has been inaugurated by people called by God and filled with the Spirit to speak out against the corrosion and corruption that destroys the life of God's people.

Christ died because he proclaimed the truth loud and clear, the truth about the cant and the hypocrisy of his 'superiors' who presided over the religious tradition into which he had been born. Do we accuse him of spreading scandal by making known the immoral behaviour of these religious leaders to whom the ordinary people had looked for spiritual inspiration and leadership? Do we accuse him of being uncharitable for likening them to a brood of vipers, for calling them whited sepulchres full of decay and corruption, and many other things beside?

You see, if reform is to come into the Church at this epoch-making moment in her history it must begin as it always has begun in the past, by the proclamation of the truth no matter what that may cost – and you can be sure it will cost much. It's time to face for ourselves truths that the secular world is bringing into the open anyway, as the media unearths scandal after scandal, shocking the very people from whom the Church authorities have been trying to hide the truth. Of course there are many good men and women in the Church, just as there were many genuine religious leaders in the time of Jesus, but sadly their impact has not been strong enough to prevent the corruption of their peers.

As the political philosopher Edmund Burke once said, 'That evil may prevail it is enough that good men do nothing', or words to that effect. It could also be added that when they try to do something they are marginalised, discredited and forced out of their respective orders, or silenced in some other way.

This is what has happened to so many young priests and religious, who were burning to live and proclaim the 'new theology' that fired them with enthusiasm for the simple message of the gospel, as that message had first fired the early Christians. They sincerely wanted to turn the dream of Pope John into reality by adapting the message that had so inspired them to the needs of the modern world. However, more of this next time.

Love,
David

4

Just an Old Man's Dream?

Dear Susanna,
You're absolutely right; that's exactly what Pope John wanted to do. When one of the Cardinals heard that he was going to call a Second Vatican Council when he should have been making his will and saying his prayers, he said, 'Surely, Holy Father, it's too soon.' To which the Pope replied, 'I was beginning to think it was too late.' When the same Cardinal asked why he was calling such a Council, Pope John opened a window and said, 'To let some fresh air into the room.'

Contemporary commentators interpreted this fresh air as nothing other than the breath of God's own Spirit who drew life out of chaos at the beginning of time and breathed life into a new Church at the first Pentecost. When Pope John made a pilgrimage to the Holy Land those same commentators interpreted his visit as a profound symbolic action summing up all he aimed to do in the Council that few of his close advisers in the Roman Curia thought necessary.

The renewal that would be introduced by the Council would involve stepping over almost two thousand years of complexity in order to return to the simplicity of the early Christian Church inspired by the gospels. Here the principles of Christian theology, liturgy and spirituality would be rediscovered in all their primitive purity, then adapted to the needs of the Church in the twentieth century.

Thanks to the many great biblical theologians and liturgists whose master works preceded the Council it was in itself a great success, but it never had the deep and lasting effect on the Church that Pope John had originally hoped for.

I was a student during the period shortly before the Council, as ignorant of what came to be called the 'new theology' as the professors who taught me. But everything changed when two fellow students, both Cambridge graduates, returned from their holidays on the continent, one from Germany, the other from France. They were brimming over with enthusiasm for the exciting new theology that had inspired them and with which they began to inspire us.

We devoured book after book of the new, exhilarating theology, leaving until what was called 'swot week' at the end of term the cramming of the boring old Latin textbooks necessary to pass our exams and satisfy our tutors. They for their part were not only ignorant of, but actively opposed to, the ideas that set us all afire. The open warfare that divided the students from the teachers continued after ordination as the young priests found themselves isolated in religious houses or presbyteries where there was little sympathy, and sometimes open hostility, towards the ideals that had in fact been sanctioned by the Council. Despite this ignorance their seniors and their superiors were nevertheless forced to implement the new ideas.

In obedience they reluctantly obeyed, but as many of them did not understand the theology behind the changes and as they were unwilling to allow the younger priests who did to explain it, the laity were left confused and the young priests themselves frustrated. I remember feeling utterly despondent myself when our parish priest stood up to introduce the new changes with the words, 'All you have to do is to learn to become a "jack-in-the-box", jumping up and down as the new rubrics tell you'. You may well remember him and that particular sermon, because he was your parish priest too at the time and the chaplain of your junior school. Now I know where you get some of your strange ideas!

No reason for anything was given because the reasons were not known or not understood. Through ignorance rather than malice the majority of priests of the older generation dug in their heels. The laity became ever more confused and began to vote with their feet, as did so many of the younger clergy who became more and more frustrated and therefore disillusioned. Sadly the voting has gone on and today there are fewer practising Catholics than Anglicans in the UK and fewer priests to serve them since long before the war. I'm not writing this in an attempt to apportion blame, but to try to pinpoint the problem that has prevented the vision and the hope of Pope John being realised as deeply as many would have hoped. As Monsignor Ronald Knox once said, 'the more clearly you are able to pinpoint the problem the more clearly you are able to see the solution'.

I know that the end of the second millennium and the beginning of the third is purely an artificial and even inaccurate date in Christian chronology, but it could be an important symbolic moment. It could herald a new departure for all who wish to be kindled afresh with the Spirit of Christ, the Spirit that transformed the first Christians at the beginning of the first millennium.

Love,
David

5

The Dream Fades

Dear Susanna,
Yes, you're right, that's precisely what happened. It was the ignorant intransigence of their seniors and their superiors who steadfastly opposed the spirit of the Council that so frustrated the younger generation of priests. They felt helpless because they were prevented from communicating what so fired them.

While implementing the new rules and regulations that they felt were forced upon them, without giving the explanations that were beyond them, the old guard succeeded in confusing the laity. The laity for their part could do no more than agree with their disgruntled pastors or vote with their feet. They were confused and bewildered, and the clergy did little if anything to make the faith they were brought up in of any relevance to the new world in which they found themselves. The younger generation of priests who had the knowledge to implement the spirit of the Council began to leave in ever-increasing numbers, not just because they were marginalised and frustrated, but because of something further that had been denied them.

For important historical reasons that I will explain later, both the younger and the older generation of priests and religious had been starved of the profound mystical experience of God, without which celibates will have difficulty in functioning for long without noticeable moral decline. In the case of the young priests this meant that the frustration that isolated them made them yearn for the support and consolation that few had ever been taught to find in God. Inevitably they began to seek it elsewhere.

The older generation suffered too because many had never developed a prayer life much beyond the early beginnings. They were not sufficiently open to the action of the Spirit, who would have enabled them to see with clarity what had inspired Pope John. It would have enabled them to see the essence of the new biblical theology that was rooted in the Risen Christ and the simplicity of the gospel message even though they could not assimilate it in detail overnight. As Jesus promised at the Last Supper, the Holy Spirit whom he sent would have united both young and old enabling them to work together to bring about the profound spiritual reform for which Pope John had been inspired to call the Council. The failure of seminaries and religious orders to guide those whom they trained towards the experiential love of God meant that the decline in religious standards that already preceded the Council was accelerated. Instead of leading to greater responsibility for personal spiritual growth and a corresponding quality of service for the laity, the new freedoms offered by the Council's decisions led to licence for which the Council itself was later blamed. Even those who were staunchly against the spirit of the Council were happy enough to make use of the new freedoms that it offered them, but they regularly misused them for their own personal comfort and pleasure.

Although I would argue that much of the religious practice of priests and religious before the Council had degenerated into formalism, it did at least help maintain a certain external personal discipline and even impressed outsiders who couldn't see beyond appearances. However, after the Council, when so much of the formalism was swept away in pursuit of greater personal responsibility, that shift was seen as a licence for personal freedom with few constraints. So many of the young who left did so not just because they were prevented from communicating to others what meant so much to them, or because they sought the consolation elsewhere that they should have found in God, but for another reason. They became more and more scandalised by the irreligious behaviour of many of those who opposed them in the name of orthodoxy and in the name of a more traditional way of religious life. That way of life seemed to have done little for most of those who clung to the past and they seemed only too pleased to cast it aside when it suited them. It would be false, therefore, to presume that the bad eggs left whilst the good eggs remained. It goes without saying that all this had its effect on the laity and on vocations to the priesthood and the religious life, and I will return to this theme later.

Love,
David

6

A Culture of Confusion

Dear Susanna,
What you say is true. As the years have gone by so much of what shocked those who left has begun to upset insiders too, laity who were once inclined to treat as sour grapes stories that have since been confirmed, not just by the popular press, but by the courts of law.

Far too many cases have hit the headlines to deceive all but the most naive into believing that they are rare, isolated instances of behaviour that any lay statistician can see speaks of many more such cases. More of the same magnitude or even greater have evaded detection, and others of lesser magnitude that may not be considered important enough to titillate newspaper readers. However, they are important enough to contribute to the spiritual decline of the ecclesiastical institutions to which those involved belong.

It is simply untrue to suggest that several generations of young people have not responded to the call to the priesthood or the religious life just because the materialism of the world around them has seduced them. The young of every generation are notoriously idealistic and have in the past felt drawn to the priesthood and the religious life in large numbers. It is unfair to blame them when they fail to see the ideals to which they aspire embodied there.

As you may know, I spent much of my time in the 1980s giving talks to and listening to young men and women who were in training for the priesthood and the religious life. I was deeply moved and impressed by their idealism, but deeply saddened by their failure to find the idealism to which they aspired embodied in the religious orders to which they had committed themselves. The reason why there are so few vocations is not because today's young lack idealism but because, for the most part, they do not find in the priesthood or the religious life what inspired previous generations. Before moving on to show what I feel must be done to change this sad state of affairs I want to say something about how all these different factors have had such a devastating effect on the laity.

I remember talking to Captain Feehan, the founder of The Mercier Press, in Cork, shortly after the Council. He was a highly intelligent man who, before the Council, had his finger on the pulse of current theological opinion as a major publisher of theological and spiritual books. However, as a layman without any knowledge of the 'new theology' that was rampant on the continent, he found himself all at sea and his business all but on the rocks because he simply didn't know what to publish. He had to change direction almost overnight, choosing to publish secular works rather than the religious books for which he had originally founded his famous publishing house. If this is what happened to the green wood, whatever would happen to the dry?

Ninety-five per cent of Catholics hadn't a clue what was going on at the Council and they were therefore dependent on priests for the guidance that simply wasn't given. Few schools had teachers who were able to understand and hand on to the young something of Pope John's dream for reforming the Church at the end of the twentieth century.

You'll well remember that after the Council my whole time was spent working for the young, first at Ivy Lodge, the youth centre that I founded in what was then your parish at Woodford Green. Then from the late sixties to the early eighties I ran Walsingham House, the residential centre at Chingford where you came with your school for one of the many courses I gave to school groups week in week out, year after year. And I was continually horrified at the standard of religious education taught at the vast majority of Catholic schools that sent children to us from all over the Westminster and Brentwood dioceses. As I hosted and then attended Catholic educational conferences I discovered that my experience was not unique, but matched by others involved in education throughout the country. Everywhere there was confusion that was reflected in the children's learning. They were simply fed up with learning about the religion that just bored them and seemed totally irrelevant to their lives.

I'm sure you remember what it was like when you came with your classmates to Walsingham House. I had great difficulty in introducing any religious theme without hearing barely suppressed moans and groans that forced me to express myself in sociological or pseudo-scientific language rather than spiritual. But, of course, your class was quite different! Till next time.

Love,
David

7

A Fatal Flaw

Dear Susanna,
Perhaps it wasn't all black, it was just that it seemed so at the time! Occasionally I was delighted to discover exceptional schools or exceptional teachers, but they were very unusual.

Sometimes I would come across a parish run by an enlightened and committed parish priest whose influence on the young was so great that I could tell them before they told me what parish they came from. The Benedictine Parish at Cockfosters was such a place and Dom. Edmund Jones was such a priest. But in others it was heartbreaking to see young people being put off the faith that all too many would cast aside within years of finishing their education. As the eighties ran their course I have to admit that I lost track of the Catholic education that had dismayed me in the seventies, but to this day I have not heard much to convince me that things have got radically better.

The vast number of young priests who left the priesthood and the even greater number of women who left the religious life was confirmation – if confirmation were needed – that the so-called 'new theology' was not only wrong, but positively dangerous, according to its critics. These reactionaries therefore retired into a sort of complacent conservatism that idealised the pre-Vatican Church, whilst accepting its practical relaxations. To so many of those who should know better the Council is simply seen as a strange inexplicable aberration of the sixties.

Since becoming a journalist I have been able to mix with a wide variety of Catholic intelligentsia, whom for the most part have all astounded me by their general theological conservatism. The older generation educated before the Council seem hardly touched by it and their younger counterparts seem to have fallen for an idealised pre-Vatican Church that never actually existed. I am, of course, only generalising. Thankfully there are many exceptions. But in general I find that whether such people are labelled as left or right wing, liberal or progressive, they seem to have one thing in common: they are ignorant of the exciting biblical theology that set my generation of students alight.

Now this gives me the opportunity to correct a misunderstanding. If I have given you the impression that if only those priests and religious who left had stayed behind then Pope John's dream would have long since been realised, then I have misled you. It by no means follows. Sadly two factors in their training, that they shared with the older generation, would have either prevented them from doing this or made it very difficult to do it adequately. The first was that they suffered from a fatal flaw in their spiritual training. For important historical reasons that I have already hinted at and which I will explain in detail later, a proper understanding of and preparation for the mystical experience of God's love through prayer was sadly absent. This would have complemented their celibacy and enabled them to be more open to the action of the Holy Spirit, who alone could have united all in bringing about a new Pentecost as he had brought about the first. The second factor was that, like their predecessors, they had undergone a classical education which inevitably meant that they studied biblical theology while wearing Greek-tinted spectacles and so misread it. It became for all too many of them another, if more acceptable, intellectual system to be studied and understood primarily with the mind.

Although they believed that they understood it they were deceiving themselves, because it could only be fully understood with the heart and not by the mind alone. For Jesus and his disciples, who were Jews, the heart does not simply mean the seat of the emotions, but rather the whole person – mind and spirit, body and soul. When St John said at the end of his gospel that he had written it so that we can come to know the Lord Jesus Christ, he meant knowing him in the biblical sense, not in the Greek sense. In other words, he wrote his theology of Jesus so that we can come to enter into him by the power of the same Holy Spirit who raised him from the dead. The only way to do this is through the ever-deepening prayer leading to contemplation that has for centuries been omitted from the training of priests and religious. It is not sufficient to celebrate the sacred mysteries that make Christ present to us day by day unless we develop the inner openness in prayer that enables us to be taken up into Christ. The more we enter into him the more we begin to see and understand everything with the same wisdom that filled him. I do hope all this makes sense to you. I know what I want to say, but sometimes I think I may be over-complicating what I'm trying to clarify!

Love,
David

8

A Classical Mind-set

Dear Susanna,
The Vatican Council mainly failed then for two reasons. First, the vast majority of those who were presented with the new theology simply failed to understand it. (I will return to and explain this theme later.) In general, the older generation simply couldn't understand, or couldn't be bothered, or were too set in their ways. Secondly, those, mainly the younger generation, who thought they could understand were deceiving themselves, because their understanding was only superficial. They too were blinkered by the same cultural mind-set as the older generation. That's why, although they had a far more comprehensive understanding of it, their understanding was still fatally flawed. They only understood it primarily with their mind, not with their hearts, and not with the biblical knowledge that would alone draw them into the One in whom all theology is embodied as wisdom.

Now I would like to make it quite clear that some of the greatest saints knew little if anything about what later came to be called 'the new theology'. The scholarship open to us was simply not open to them, but by entering into Christ, through prayer to contemplation, they came to know and experience all that anyone needs to know. This is why, while the Vatican Council failed to fulfil what it promised, the Council of Trent, which was held in the middle of the sixteenth century, was successful. At that time there were many saints, founders of new religious orders and reformers of old ones, without whom the Council would not have been called let alone succeeded.

Before the Council of Trent the prevailing theology was scholastic. In other words, it was rooted in the Greek philosophical mind-set that prevented later generations understanding the biblical theology. However it was saved from becoming a pure intellectualism by a vibrant spirituality centred on the humanity of Jesus, thanks largely to St Bernard and St Francis of Assisi. Under the influence of the great saints and mystics of the period, meditation on the humanity of Jesus led on into mystical contemplation. It was here that the wisdom was learnt to integrate a Christ-centred spirituality with a Greek-based theology in a satisfactory synthesis that was lacking several centuries after the Council of Trent. This latter state of affairs was still prevailing immediately before the Second Vatican Council, so ensuring its failure.

If only the Vatican Council had had its St Philip Neri whose spiritual direction, wisdom and personal holiness did so much to sanctify the curia who served the Council of Trent. If it had only had lay organisations like 'The Oratory of Divine Love' and new and reformed religious orders like the Theatines, the Barnabites, the Capuchins, the Carmelites and not least the Jesuits, things might have been different. These orders and organisations produced men and women of wisdom and holiness, who not only helped bring about the Council of Trent, but also helped spread its reform so successfully.

The Vatican Council was preceded by decades of invaluable biblical and liturgical scholarship and the influence of innumerable scholars of distinction, but so much of their work has failed to bear the practical fruit that was promised. The lack of spiritual training that affected both them and their enthusiastic followers meant that their new and exciting theology remained, unlike that of their Tridentine counterparts, predominantly intellectual. Although it tried to supersede the dry scholastic theology that had long since passed its sell-by date, it only succeeded in causing confusion amongst the clergy and this was reflected in the laity. But more of this next time.

Love,
David

9

Mind the Gap!

Dear Susanna,

That's quite true – the confusion amongst the laity is only a mirror of the confusion found amongst the clergy. Some still aspire to the 'new theology', other amateur DIY theologians have concocted their own synthesis by cherry-picking from the old and the new according to their own individual idiosyncrasies, whilst others have retreated into a neo-conservatism.

Now when any theology becomes detached from spirituality and the profound prayer that opens us to the same Spirit from which Jesus received his wisdom, a gap quickly opens between theory and practice. When this begins to happen and outsiders start to see a discrepancy between what is preached and what is practised, religious leaders often try to hide what they cannot remedy. Then slowly but surely they are forced to adopt the cover-up tactics that I mentioned before, for fear of being labelled as hypocritical leaders of a hypocritical religion. Once again the truth has to be recognised before change can take place. Then it has to be realised that change cannot be brought about by one's own endeavour but only by God's. When this is understood then reform can begin as repentance opens a person to the only One who can give the power to practise what is preached. This is why every single successful reform movement in the Church's history has been brought about by a response to the Holy Spirit speaking through men and women, who call people to repentance, to turn back to God through prayer.

Whenever any religious system prevails which is predominantly 'intellectual' it creates not only a gap between theory and practice but a gap between those who think they are the intellectuals at the top and the ordinary run-of-the-mill people at the bottom. In short, it tends to become elitist. It comprises those who think they are 'in the know' and those who aren't. This gap has been exacerbated since the Vatican Council as different theological theories have prevailed amongst the clergy and the Catholic intelligentsia. The inevitable result of this is that the ordinary man or woman in the pew is continually confused and frustrated. Even if they are able to find satisfactory explanations of the faith, few of the clergy are able to give the spiritual help for which they crave. Sheep without shepherds tend to disperse, searching by themselves for food and nourishment, but with varying degrees of success.

Many, particularly of the older generation, find comfort and satisfaction in the devotions that they learnt at their mother's knee. Others find great comfort, inspiration and strength from visiting places where apparitions are said to have taken place and supernatural signs have been seen. Still others join prayer groups, in particular the charismatic prayer groups that seem to have grown from strength to strength since the sixties when they first made such an impact within the Catholic Church. Some people may draw strength from several of these things.

Now there's nothing wrong with traditional methods of piety; I was brought up on them myself and still regularly return to them. However, it has to be admitted that they are not as readily acceptable to the young of this generation as they were to the young of mine. It's not for me to pronounce on the latest apparitions when the Church has not endorsed them, but one has to say that the most recent events that have happened at Medjugorje, for instance, seem to have done nothing but good. The simple message that is received seems to be nothing other than the same timeless message of the gospel. As a Vincentian priest once said to me, how else could God reach out to ordinary simple folk amid such contemporary confusion to restate the same message that Jesus preached? Nor should we be surprised that signs are used as Jesus used them himself to help guarantee the origin and authenticity of a message that might not be received without them.

Charismatic prayer is nothing other than the prayer of serious-minded believers coming together to pass through, as a group, the first fervour that was traditionally experienced behind the closed doors of a personal prayer life. Inevitably group emotion generates psychological phenomena that are often given a theological rather than a psychological explanation. However, I am convinced that such prayer has an important part to play in the profound spiritual reform that I hope will characterise the beginning of the new millennium.

Love,
David

10

Preparing for the Future

Dear Susanna,
I admit that charismatic renewal does tend to attract people with psychological problems, but is there no place in the Church for such people? Who else welcomes them into their midst? I know that many who do not belong to the movement themselves find the enthusiasm of charismatics embarrassing and their spiritual arrogance a little disconcerting, but they are after all spiritual adolescents. Is there no place in the Church for them either? You can't have adults without them first being adolescents, as you're going to find out to your cost very soon now!

All the great mystics have shown through their writings how the faults of spiritual adolescents gradually disappear as they are led onwards through purification and into contemplative prayer. Anyone who has taken the trouble to study the theology that is at the heart of the charismatic movement will have seen that it is both orthodox and authentic, confirming that it is indeed the Holy Spirit who is at work leading beginners onwards towards mystical prayer. The sadness is that the very people who should be helping these beginners stay well away. They have never developed a serious prayer life themselves that would enable them to understand what is happening and give the required help and support that is needed. Therefore they tend to remain aloof, looking down on those whom they sometimes call 'charimaniacs', with their pseudo-

Greek rationalism, as unable to help such people as they are unable to help themselves.

The question must now be asked as to how we can do our part to bring about the deepest desire of Christ himself, which he prayed for so passionately at the Last Supper – 'that they may all be one' (John 17:21–23). In other words, where do we go from the confusion that we see everywhere in the Church in order to bring about a genuine Christian restoration that is well overdue?

I must admit that in this matter I am a conservative. However, I do not belong to the particular brand of pseudo-conservatism that thrives amongst some of the clergy I meet and many of the Catholic intelligentsia whom I tend to meet through my work. All too many of them think that they are traditionalists when in fact they subscribe to their own fanciful brand of traditionalism that never in fact existed. It gives its own particular spin to a distorted Tridentine theology that was in desperate need of renewal both before and after the Second World War, hence the scholastic renewal that failed during the fifties. I suppose it was inevitable that those who, for whatever reason, chose to reject the Vatican Council had nowhere else to go other than to the threadbare Tridentine theology that preceded it.

G.K. Chesterton perfectly described the sort of conservatism to which I subscribe when he said that every true conservative must be a revolutionary, on the simple principle that if you paint a room white and you want it to remain white you must continually repaint it. This was the symbolic meaning of Pope John's visit to the Holy Land, symbolising what the Council he called was intended to do. Using the latest biblical scholarship that had never before been available to the Church, the principles of Christian theology, liturgy and pastoral practice would be studied anew at source. Then in his own words, 'reading the signs of the times in which we live', these principles should be applied in such a way that the Church could be renewed according to the heart and mind of Christ. This means that we must re-examine and study the work of the great biblical and liturgical scholars in order to understand the purpose of the Council. This must then be implemented along with the explanations that were never adequately given before.

The enormity of this task is exacerbated by the fact that scholarship did not stand still after the Vatican Council, nor did the world for which it was called. The 'signs of the times' at the beginning of the third millennium are substantially different from those that existed in the 1960s. Nevertheless this task must be undertaken if the Church's ever-diminishing effectiveness is to be arrested and reversed. We need the salt to give it savour, the leaven to help it rise, so that it becomes what it had originally been made for – the place where God's glory is embodied in those who inhabit it. For, as St Irenaeus once said, 'the greatest glory to God on earth is man fully alive'. However, something further is required this time round to prevent the failure to achieve renewal as happened the first time. Everybody concerned, from the greatest scholar to the simplest of the faithful, must try to enter into the heart and mind of Christ through an ever-deepening prayer life. This alone will enable the Holy Spirit to give us the insight to see what must be done and the power to do it. Only the Holy Spirit will save us from the deep confusion that we are in at present, and bring us back to the unity for which Christ prayed at the Last Supper. As prayer deepens and ripens in contemplation, it automatically draws all who pray together, as they are drawn ever more fully into the heart and mind of Christ.

Although we must all begin together without delay, it is of particular importance that all those who are being trained to lead and guide us into the twenty-first century must be trained first and foremost in prayer. This will enable them to understand biblical theology with the heart as well as the mind. That's why prayer must be taught and be given pride of place in all seminars and houses of study.

This does not mean that we have to ignore the scholastic theology that is part of our Christian heritage. It will always be needed to understand some of the finer points of theological speculation. However, it must be seen as ancillary to biblical theology, which alone will enable us to understand the principles of Christian life and liturgy at source. Nor must it be used in such a way that confuses what must always be the fundamental theology of our faith that is rooted in Christ and in its first expression in the Early Church. Who are the main theologians, then, to whom we must look to guide us into the future – St Thomas Aquinas or John Duns Scotus, perhaps, or more modern theologians like Karl Rahner, Edward Schillebeeckx or one of the many liberation theologians? No, none of these, or rather all of these, but only in so far as they enable us to understand and cherish the authentic teachings of the first and most important theologians of all – Matthew, Mark, Luke and John, and of course Peter and Paul and the other writers whose works comprise what we call the New Testament. All these men were theologians, but theologians with a difference. For a start almost all of them had spent many months, if not several years, in the company of Jesus whilst he was on earth. Then they were saints, and finally they were divinely inspired in all that they wrote. This gives them more than a head start on any later theologians. Understanding them means understanding the cultural milieu that formed them and the man to whom their writings bear witness.

If all Christians, whatever their origins, could only divest themselves of the denominational baggage that encumbers them for long enough to go back to study their origins in this way, the future would be assured. However, the study must be accompanied not just with prayers but with the deep daily sustained prayer that will alone enable the fire of the Holy Spirit to purge the pride and prejudice that blinds the bigot in us all to the truth. Then under the influence of the same Spirit, who inspired the scriptures in the first place, we will be able to see their true meaning as never before.

Although we may seem poles apart at the beginning of this process we will soon find ourselves automatically drawing together as we draw ever closer to Christ, like the spokes of a wheel as they draw closer to the cog. Endless ecumenical dialogue has got us nowhere in the last forty years but round and round in circles. True, it has made us less intolerant than before and even fostered cross-denominational friendships that were unheard of before, but we're no nearer the unity that Christ prayed for. Only the Holy Spirit can bring about this unity, by opening the eyes of all who would receive him, to enable them to reread and understand the scriptures, inspired by the Holy Spirit, with the true wisdom that alone can unite all in the love of Christ. Only then will the unity of all Christians be a sign to the world of the greater unity of all humankind in the love for which Christ came. This is the ultimate goal to which all Christians are called. Although I am speaking to you of the need for and the principles that should govern a 'Christian Renaissance' in the context of the Catholic Church, this 'Renaissance' can only be as successful as Christ wished if each individual Christian denomination does likewise. All Christians must have the humility to face the truth of their own failure to live the gospel as they should, and then to ask for the grace to 'repent' by turning back, not to the Christ we've fashioned in the image and likeness of our own bias and bigotry, but to Christ as he is in himself. For he is the living source of the only love that can unite us all as one family. Well, that'll have to do for now – I've already written a longer letter than usual!

Love,
David

11

A Second Renaissance

Dear Susanna,

Perhaps what I'm trying to say will become clearer if I explain a little more fully what I mean by the 'new theology'. It engenders a totally new approach to studying the faith. It involves making use of the latest research in biblical studies to see and understand the faith in the context of the Jewish culture in which Jesus first communicated the 'good news'. Then, with the help of new discoveries in archaeology and historical research, it studies the way in which the early Christians understood and practised their faith, throwing new light on the essential principles of Christianity that have become unnecessarily confused and complicated over subsequent centuries.

The 'new theology', then, involves nothing other than a second Renaissance. If the first Renaissance involved rediscovering the glories of the Greco-Roman world, this second Renaissance involves rediscovering the glories of the Judaeo-Christian world. Like its predecessor, this Christian Renaissance does not intend to recreate the past in the present exactly, but first to study anew the context and culture in which Jesus first preached the 'good news' and in which it was first practised; then secondly, seeing the principles of the Christian faith anew in all their original purity, to apply and, where necessary, adapt them to the world in which we live today.

It has been easier for the younger generation to do this, because they approached it with uncluttered minds and also because they had time on their side. Understandably the older generation were too busy with their pastoral work to put their minds to studying a wholly new approach to theology on their own, although some tried and some succeeded. Moreover, even if they had the time and the intellectual wherewithal to attempt it, it was still not easy. You see, they had all been brought up in a cultural mind-set that, thanks to the first Renaissance, was predominantly Greek. This standpoint was reinforced when they studied scholastic theology in the seminary that depended largely on a philosophy that was predominantly Greek too and quite different from the Jewish way of thinking. Nobody can question the subtle intellectual heritage that we owe to the Greeks, nor should it ever be cast aside, but neither can anyone deny that it was through the profound mystical heritage of the Jews that God chose to communicate his truth to the world. That's why, now that modern studies have enabled a Christian Renaissance to take place, an authentic biblical theology must henceforth take pride of place. At the same time scholastic theology will always be needed to help us understand and explain the more sophisticated aspects of the Christian faith. One must, in future, be at the service of the other: the scholastic at the service of the biblical and not vice versa. Nor should an attempt be made to fuse the two together because two totally different cultures into one will not go, as I found out for myself.

Shortly before the Vatican Council, a brilliant theologian who had recently finished his studies in Rome was appointed to teach us theology. The student body was delighted, for although he had had a classical education at school like the rest of us and a scholastic education in the seminary, he had also been able to study the new biblical theology that excited us. However, although he had a brilliant mind he had been unable to fuse the old theology with the new, to his or to anyone else's satisfaction. You see, each represented a different way of understanding and expressing the truth.

The Greeks were 'essentialists', the Jews 'existentialists'. In other words, the Greek mind wants to know the inner nature of everything, what it is in itself. The Jewish mind is more interested in what a thing does, how it acts. The first is primarily theoretical, the second practical. Ask a Greek, for instance, what a neighbour is and he will say, 'A neighbour is . . .' – in other words, he tries to give a definition of 'neighbourliness'. However, when you ask a Jew what a neighbour is, he will say, 'There was a man travelling on the road to Jericho, who was set upon by robbers . . .' – in other words, he will give you a practical example of neighbourliness, so that you can learn how to be a good neighbour too.

In the same way, while the Greek is interested in trying to define exactly what God is in himself, the Jew is more concerned with what God does. If a Greek came to believe that God is love he would try to define it, whilst a Jew would try to understand how to receive it. We used to joke that if our theology professor was faced with two doors, one of which said 'Heaven', the other 'A lecture on heaven', he would choose the lecture every time. In other words, he only understood the 'new theology' as an outsider, as a Greek seeking purely intellectual knowledge.

This leads me to another important point that must be recognised by anyone who genuinely wants to understand Christianity through the 'new theology'. It is not primarily an intellectualism but a mysticism. It is not concerned just with understanding what God is in himself, but about receiving and experiencing the love that pours out continually through Jesus and responding to it in kind. If it is to be understood as intended, it must be understood with the heart. For Jesus and his fellow Jews the heart does not mean just the seat of the emotions, but the whole person from the mind to the inmost recesses of the personality. In effect, it has to be experienced as Jesus himself experienced it, as it possessed every part of him.

Love cannot be understood by the mind alone but by experience. That's why from the beginning prayer to contemplation was always seen as the only way to explore the mystery of God at work in us. This is why one of the great desert fathers and one of the first great mystical theologians, Evagrius Pontus, said, 'A theologian is a man of prayer and a man of prayer is a theologian.'

Love,
David

12

Going Native

Dear Susanna,
That's precisely why you had such difficulty teaching religion in Singapore. The faith, as you knew it, had been explained in the context of the Greek culture in which you have been brought up. That meant that you had to either convert your pupils to European culture in order to explain it or be converted to theirs so that you could translate your faith into their language and culture.

It seems incredible, but not all missionaries have taken the trouble to do what you did, though it's obvious from what you say that you've found this out for yourself! Some have done, but they are as often as not viewed as oddities by their fellows for 'going native' and somehow letting the side down. After all, one has to have standards and the standards are European, as was the way they chose to explain and communicate the Christianity that they preached. People could not fully understand it as they did unless they were first Europeanised and re-educated in the Western Neo-classical style.

I remember spending many evenings talking to my sister-in-law, who is a Zulu, about the traditional culture and way of life of her people. I was astounded at how close this is to the culture of the ancient Jews and how far removed they both are from the Greco-Roman presentation of Christianity to which we in the West have been accustomed. If only they could have been taught the faith as Jesus himself came to understand it, in the context of the culture he grew up in, they would easily comprehend it.

When I was in South Africa I met an anthropologist who spoke Zulu and who toured the world lecturing on Zulu culture, but he only understood it through the eyes of a Western European. His knowledge was minimal compared to that of an ordinary Franciscan priest who, with an elderly brother as his companion, had 'gone native'. He not only spoke Zulu fluently but also understood and spoke what is known as deep Zulu. It's almost a language within a language that depends on a complex use of similes and metaphors that were unknown to the anthropologist. The priest lived with the people and had completely adopted their way of life. His knowledge was that of an insider. It was both theoretical and practical. The old lay brother wasn't particularly good at the language nor could he lecture on their culture or customs, but he came to know them through a deep heartfelt love that is the only knowledge that ultimately matters.

The way the anthropologist understood Zulu culture is the way many have come to know about the culture of the ancient Jews, never truly understanding it. Whereas love of the people he was serving enabled the Franciscan priest to discard the mind-set in which he had been brought up and put on theirs instead. He was able to study their culture from the inside and so understand it as it really is. Although he was no scripture scholar, when he settled amongst the Zulu people his knowledge and love of their way of life sent him back to study the culture in which the gospel had first been communicated. He was astounded to discover that it was far closer to the Zulu culture than the one in which he'd been brought up and it enabled him to teach the gospel message far more effectively than before. The brother who lived with him hadn't the time or the wherewithal to study in detail the people he came to know better than anyone, because he loved them as they were and lived among them as one of them. This quality of love is transcultural.

It is the knowledge of the anthropologist that has predominated since the Vatican Council amongst most theologians and scripture scholars. It is useful knowledge, but it is not enough. It is primarily the theoretical knowledge of outsiders for whom knowledge often becomes an end in itself. We need more theologians and priests who are able to 'go native' and understand the Semitic culture and way of life that formed Jesus himself and his first followers; this will enable them to be open to the same love that filled Jesus. In turn, we can relearn through them the simple gospel message in all its pristine purity. We can't all study as theologians do, but we can all learn to love like that simple Franciscan lay brother, loving the man who embodied the Jewish culture that formed him and enabled him to communicate God's love to all who would receive it. This is the stuff that all the saints were made of, because it is the true wisdom that ultimately transcends all other forms of knowledge. The vast majority of them knew little about the Semitic culture that determined the way in which Jesus expressed the 'good news'. But by entering into him through love they learnt all that was necessary, for they learnt 'the one thing necessary' which surpasses all understanding and unites all people of every race and culture.

Love,
David

13

True Wisdom

Dear Susanna,

I'm afraid I must disagree with you. The gospel message isn't difficult or complicated to understand at all. Sadly it's we human beings who have complicated what was so simple to understand when Jesus and the apostles first proclaimed it. They met opposition not because nobody could understand them but because what they preached seemed so unbelievable. However, after centuries of trying to understand and express the gospel according to a Greek cultural mindset and then endlessly trying to explain and defend it against those who would distort it, you can't be blamed for thinking that you've got to have half a dozen degrees in theology to understand it. What was originally simple and clear became progressively more complex.

You see, precisely because the Greek philosophers and their followers didn't believe that God could have any interest in them, they had to go it alone and work out everything for themselves. That's why they developed a highly intellectual way of life. The Jews, on the other hand, had a God who was not only interested in them but who entered into every aspect of their lives, showing them where they were going and giving them guidelines on how to get there. They didn't need to work out everything for themselves or develop a sophisticated intellectual approach to every aspect of life.

Subsequently, when large numbers of Greek intellectuals

were converted to Christianity they used their sharpened minds to understand their new faith ever more deeply. What was wrong with that? Nothing at all; hadn't St Peter himself encouraged it? The trouble was that some of them didn't know when to stop. Everything possible had to be defined, to be explained in detail to the very limits of human understanding. Now it has to be admitted that the precise and subtle language that had been sharpened by Greek philosophy proved an invaluable tool. It helped to express the faith with greater precision than before and so defend it against heresy in early times – and in later times, for that matter – and that is well and good. However, it is not well and good that the Greek presentation of the faith began to make Christianity into a highly intellectual religion that seemed a long way removed from the simple message that Jesus preached and taught to the ordinary work-a-day folk who followed him. Furthermore, its continual use to counteract heresy meant that it tended to stress those articles of faith that had been denied by heretics, so distorting the faith and giving a complex and negative expression to what Jesus had preached so simply and positively.

I was saved from this over complication by what I now see as my greatest gift, which is my dyslexia. As none of my teachers understood me and wrote me off as either bone-headed or bone-idle I couldn't look to them for help. I had no option, therefore, but to look elsewhere. I thought that if no human being could understand me, maybe God would. That's why I turned to prayer. That's why I continued to pray when other people might have given up. They had somewhere else to go; I hadn't. They could turn to their books, to their studies, to fulfil the ambitions that my dyslexia denied to me. I didn't press on in prayer because I was particularly pious but because I was particularly needy. Frankly, I had no one else to turn to. What I had originally thought was my greatest weakness became my greatest strength. When I came to study the 'new theology' it enabled me to see with ever-increasing simplicity what had seemed so complex before.

Believe me, I'm not anti-intellectual, but I am against the sort of Greco-Christian intellectualism that has all too often stifled the simple gospel message over the centuries. If I may paraphrase the imitation of Christ, I would rather know how to experience the love of God than how to understand it, though I'd like to understand it too as much as I am able. But as William of St Thierry once said, 'You'll never really know someone unless you love them'. It's exactly the same with God, as the mystics found out from their own experience. They discovered that the most sublime knowledge which is wisdom, comes from God through the love that surpasses the understanding. This other-worldly love is experienced in profound mystical prayer, as the saints have discovered. This is what St Augustine, St Bernard, St Thomas Aquinas and the other true Christian intellectuals finally found out for themselves, and pass on to those who are able to learn from them. True wisdom does not precede love, it comes through it. Moreover, that love is received in prayer, as every authentic Christian thinker knows through experience.

Love,
David

14

More Mystics, Please

Dear Susanna,
Yes, it was remarkable that the Greek philosophers were able to argue for the existence of God with only reason to guide them. Moreover, you can admire their intellectual integrity when they couldn't see how God could have any interest in human beings even though he must have created them. It would be beneath him to contemplate anything less than the infinitely perfect, they believed. But this didn't mean that they had no interest in him, not by a long chalk. They believed that he was the source of all the goodness, the beauty and the truth that they desired for themselves more than anything else. If only they could be united with him they'd be able to share in these transcendental virtues and live with him for ever. However, they realised that as God had no interest in them they'd get no help from him and so they'd have to find their own way to him. The only way to be united with him, then, was to become as pure as possible by acquiring for oneself all the necessary virtues.

This is how the first Stoics were born. Stoics are people who think that they can make themselves perfect by living perfectly virtuous lives. Sadly many early Greek and Roman converts brought their stoicism with them, and this gave birth in its turn to the heresy of Pelagianism. This heresy got its name from a British monk called Pelagius; he and his disciples believed that they could acquire all virtues by their own endeavour and become the architects of their own perfection.

This had disastrous consequences by deceiving many other believers into thinking that they could obtain perfection for themselves, although the gospels made it quite clear that without God we have no power to do anything. This 'new spirituality' that came from Socrates and the Stoics, not from Jesus of Nazareth, deceived many and won them over to a sort of Christian stoicism that's been with us ever since. Although it had been smouldering under the surface all the time, it reasserted itself with a compelling urgency and power at the time of the Renaissance and its influence has remained with us ever since. To this day people claiming to be Christians still tend to think of Jesus as a great moral teacher like Socrates who came to detail the virtues that we have to acquire by our own unaided endeavour. This is a serious travesty of the truth.

Some years ago there used to be a panel programme on the radio called *The Brains Trust*, though I think it was before your time. The star of the programme was an agnostic, Cyril Edwin Joad, a Professor of Moral Philosophy. On one occasion a bishop joined him on the panel and began to wax eloquent about the moral teaching of the New Testament. 'Whether you are a believer or not,' he said, 'you must accept that Jesus has given us the most wonderful moral teaching ever taught. If only we lived by that we'd all be the better for it.'

Professor Joad's answer was immediate. 'Poppycock, rubbish,' he said. 'Jesus Christ has given the world a moral teaching that no one can possibly live by. If anyone tries to live by it, as you suggest, they will not only fail but their repeated failure will lead to utter disillusionment and despair. Go back and reread the gospel, and you'll see precisely what I mean.' He then began to quote from the gospel himself. 'The gospels say, do they not, that we should be perfect as God is perfect, that we should not only love each other as we love ourselves, but as Jesus, the supposed son of God, loves us; that we should love not only our enemies but forgive them seventy times seven, that we should further love those who would persecute and even put us to death. These moral directives would inevitably direct anyone, so misguided as to take them seriously, to disaster. They would lead to spiritual and psychological suicide unless the traveller threw in the towel, as so many do, and settled for being just a nominal Christian. The trouble with you Christians is you fill your schools, colleges, seminaries and your universities with teachers who propound a moral code that they have failed to live by themselves and which their students will also fail to live by. Inevitably they teach a way of life that's nothing but a recipe for disaster, but they simply don't see it. That's why so many of them end up guilt-ridden hypocrites.'

Well, who do you think is right – the bishop or the agnostic? I side with the agnostic and so do the gospels. The bishop would have seen this if he had only read the gospels as thoughtfully as the professor. However, even the professor hadn't read them properly or he would have seen that the gospels say many times over and in many different ways – 'Yes, I know you can't, but I can, if you only allow me.' The standards and the virtues that you find in the gospel that will alone enable a person to be united with the Father of all virtues, cannot be acquired by human endeavour alone. Only when the same Spirit who filled Jesus begins to fill us with his power will we be able to do what Jesus did, and even greater things, as he himself promised at the Last Supper.

Now I hope you can see that Christianity is not primarily a moralism but a mysticism. Its prime concern is to communicate the power to do what is quite impossible without it. This power not only enables a person to love their enemies and even those who persecute them, but those who would torture them to death, as you can read in *The Acts of the Martyrs.* There is only one way to live out the profound teachings of the gospel as Jesus did and that is to open ourselves, like him, to the one power who makes all things possible.

This power will possess you as it possessed Mary and bring Christ to birth in you. Then he can and will be able to live out the perfect Christian life again, in and through you. However, he will only be able to do this to the degree to which you allow him to make his home in you, and then return home yourself.

Love,
David

15

Christian Stoics

Dear Susanna,
I'm sorry, I wasn't trying to get at you at all! Of course I knew you'd taught for years before Michael was born, but I didn't know you taught RE. No, I don't mean to say that all teachers are no more than Christian Stoics; that would be a travesty of the truth. However, what I can only call a Greco-Roman stoicism or moralism crept back into Christian spirituality at the time of the Renaissance and it has affected us all to a greater or lesser degree ever since.

Let me explain myself. Shortly after the end of the Dark Ages when Europe was no more than an adolescent, she was married to Christianity. All marriages have their ups and downs, but by and large it was a happy marriage for many years. Then as she was moving towards middle age she fell in love with another. Divorce was all but unheard of in those days so Europe remained wedded to Christianity while flirting and finally committing adultery with a youthful pagan philosophy that was reborn at the Renaissance.

It was a philosophy that was born of Socrates, who begot Plato, who begot Aristotle, all of whom begot the Stoics and their followers in subsequent centuries down to the present day. Socrates and those who followed him were great men with great minds but sadly little faith, so, as I explained in my last letter, they could reason their way to a God who hadn't any interest in human beings. This meant, therefore, that there couldn't be any relationship with him.

No relationship, therefore no religion – for that's what the word 'religion' means, having a two-way relationship with the One who created us. If human beings really wanted to have any relationship with God it would have to be one-way traffic and it would involve tremendous human endeavour because God, contrary to Christian teaching, couldn't give any help to make it easier.

The Stoics reasoned that the only way to be united with a perfect God would be to make oneself into a perfect human being by acquiring all the necessary virtues. The man of virtue would then be in such control of himself that he would be able to free his spirit from all material things. This included his own body, which imprisoned it, so that it could be united with God who is pure spirit. These ideas, which are pagan, not Christian, were subtly reintroduced into Christian spirituality, with the best of intentions, by Christian humanists at the time of the Renaissance. They wanted to try to reform an ailing Church and rescue it from laxity and superstition before the reformers did it for them. No one was more successful at doing this in England than John Colet.

Colet was a traditional English Catholic of the old school until he studied classics, first in his own country and then in Italy at the end of the fifteenth century. There he flirted, not just with the glories of the Renaissance in general, but with the teachings of Socrates and his followers in particular. He, with his fellow humanists, thought that the Church could be saved from what threatened it by the sort of clear reasoning and virtuous living that they so admired in their classical mentors. He came back to England full of enthusiasm to share his ideas. He didn't want to share them only with his peers but with the younger generation, for whom he founded St Paul's School in London. The ideal product of this school would be embodied in a true English gentleman in whom the teachings of Socrates of Athens and Jesus of Nazareth would be perfectly harmonised. The other eight major public schools modelled themselves on St Paul's. Later public schools that were set up to accommodate the sons of the 'nouveau riche', who profited from the industrial revolution and the exploitations of empire, modelled themselves in their turn on the 'big nine'. The same aims and ideals could and still can be found in more diluted form in the grammar schools, the secondaries and in today's comprehensive schools, and sadly even in the seminaries.

I was recently amused to hear of the story of a young Jamaican boy on the radio. He'd won a scholarship to an English public school where he said he was taught to embody the morality of a fourth-century Athenian Stoic and the manners of a twentieth-century English gentleman. Catholic schools, public or otherwise, followed similar aims and ideals to their non-Catholic counterparts without even realising it, albeit with a strong diet of strictly Catholic doctrines that have never successfully effected the divorce that must separate pagan philosophy from authentic Christianity.

Just as the Greco-Roman intellectual culture cannot be successfully fused with the Judaeo-Christian, neither can their moral teaching be combined without causing considerable confusion. No one has ever conceived any moral teaching as lofty or as sublime as that which Jesus lived and preached. Nor can anybody possibly live it without being empowered to do so by the same Spirit that filled him. Before I leave this subject I must explain that, far from having any prejudice against classical Greek culture or the Renaissance that reintroduced it into European civilisation, I revelled in it as a schoolboy. It was the beginning of my love affair with the ancient world of Greece that has continued throughout my life. It was the first time I had a genuine interest in the arts and sciences and then later in philosophy, and Plato and Socrates became my heroes.

When we studied the Renaissance in the sixth form I was delighted to see just how much our European culture owed to the classical world that I had already revelled in. I am proud of that cultural heritage, of its literary, architectural and artistic masterpieces. I am proud too of all that has been achieved and all we have gained through the rise of the natural sciences and of the technology that followed in their wake. It's quite evident to me that all this would not have been possible without the endeavour of human beings who received their inspiration from the classical world of Greece and Rome. However, not even the greatest geniuses, who have achieved so much that we admire, have ever achieved the impossible.

This is precisely what is asked of us by the gospels. They don't ask us to achieve just what is humanly possible but what is morally impossible, what has only been perfectly achieved by a man who was penetrated through and through with the divine. Only by being filled with this self-same life can any human being ever hope to do likewise.

In their enthusiasm to renew the Church with the same principles that had enabled them to transform secular culture, many of the first humanists did irreparable damage to the orthodox Christian spirituality, and their legacy is still with us. As I've said before, people who have had the benefit of a classical education read the gospels with Greek-tinted spectacles and therefore misread them as I had done. Like so many others, I'd substituted Jesus for Socrates assuming that he too was primarily a great moral teacher. He had come like Socrates to educate people's moral sensibilities and to teach them the true principles and virtues on which to base their lives. I was wrong: Jesus was not primarily a philosopher or a great moral teacher but a mystic whose experience of the divine life enabled him to live a perfect human life.

Those who follow him will only be able to do the same if they open themselves to receive and experience the same divine life that he experienced. This is why he said, 'I have come that you may have life and that you may have it ever more fully' (John 10:10). In other words, he came as a mystic, not as a moralist. He came not so much to detail the way in which we should love God and serve our neighbours but to give us the power to do it. Whoever chooses to receive this power that radiates from him will also be made into a perfect human being, and then perfect human behaviour will follow as a matter of course.

Again I would emphasise that Christianity is a mysticism, not a moralism. Jesus is first a mystic, not a moral philosopher. When we understand this not just with our minds and hearts but with our whole being and begin to do something about it, we will have put aside the Christian humanism with which all too many of us were brought up. Then at last we will be on our way back to living the gospel that was lived and preached by the first Christians in imitation of the man they lived and died for.

If we have been brought up as 'bastard Christians', even though it's through no fault of our own, it's time to make ourselves legitimate once more, by returning to the unalloyed spirituality that inspired the first Christians immediately after the resurrection. What better enterprise with which to celebrate the beginning of the third millennium!

Love,
David

16

A Tragic Imbalance

Dear Susanna,
I can't help but agree with you that things would have been different if so many of the young priests and religious who believed in Vatican II and wanted to promote it hadn't left. However, even they were unable to understand it fully, for reasons that I have already hinted at, but not fully explained. The classical education that they shared with the older generation is only part of the explanation. There was another problem associated with their priestly or religious training that once again affected old and young alike. It was simply this: they had not been taught how to pray much beyond first beginnings for reasons that I must now explain in more detail. This meant that the 'new theology' that inspired them was understood only on a comparatively superficial level and never became part of their experience. That's why when they became frustrated and needed help, encouragement and support, they turned elsewhere to find what they could otherwise have received from God.

Although there aren't any reliable figures that I could quote, it was claimed at a recent seminar that several hundred thousand priests and religious, both male and female, have left since the Council. Perhaps the true figures will never be known, but they are certainly massive and call for an explanation. Although it would be impossible to determine the reason for leaving in each individual case I believe there are certain historical causes, not just explaining the numbers who have left, but the general decline in standards of those who remained. This is particularly true of those who remained in religious life, albeit with many individual exceptions.

Over four hundred years ago a renewal movement now called the 'Counter-Reformation' tried to reverse laxity within the Church and undo the harm done to orthodoxy by the Reformation. Although this movement is often associated with the Council of Trent – and that certainly canonised, strengthened and supported it – it actually began before that. As some of the older orders like the Franciscans and the Carmelites began to renew themselves from within, new orders like the Theatines and the Jesuits set new standards that had a deep and lasting influence on the Church at the time and in subsequent centuries.

Perhaps the two most influential orders after the Council of Trent were the Carmelites and the Jesuits. Under the influence of St Teresa of Avila and St John of the Cross, the Dominican school of spirituality, that stressed the action of God, reasserted itself. Once again the Carmelites emphasised how God acts in the spiritual life and, most important, in the deep contemplative prayer without which apostolic action soon falters. Under the influence of the Jesuits, the need for humanity to co-operate with God was the basis of a new form of 'apostolic spirituality', and this had a considerable impact right down to the present day.

In harness these two religious orders would have been complementary and could have brought about the renewal that the Church needed with perfect balance, but it was not to be. Sadly many would-be mystics misinterpreted the writings of St Teresa and St John, falling into the heresy of Quietism. Their over-emphasis on the action of God meant that they did virtually nothing for themselves, not even fighting against temptations. This led to gross immorality. The most infamous Quietist was a priest called Molino (b.1628), who was charged and convicted of many acts of serious sexual indecency arising from his bogus mystical teaching. Naturally the Church then came down heavily on any form of Quietism. The reaction against this heresy led to the 'anti-mystical witch hunts' whereby any form of prayer that emphasised stillness, recollection or quiet was suspect. In this climate the great Carmelite reformers came under suspicion and their teaching was either misunderstood or considered highly dangerous. The only safe path was the way of intensive activity, both in prayer and in the apostolate. In this climate the spirituality of the new Jesuit congregation was ideally suited to take the lead. Over the subsequent centuries it did sterling work bringing about renewal in the Church. However, without the emphasis that the Carmelites had once placed on contemplative prayer an imbalance crept into virtually all other religious orders.

Once the busy exhilarating prayer of first fervour fizzles out, as it always does, there was no one able to direct and guide a person onwards into the still and silent contemplative prayer that should follow it. The deep contemplative style of prayer that the older orders saw as the necessary prerequisite for successful apostolic action was understood by few, and those who did understand dared not open their mouths for fear of condemnation by the anti-mystical witch hunters.

At the beginning of prayer a person tends to form God in his or her own image and likeness and then fall in love with him through their own self-generated emotion. Contemplative prayer is quite different. It begins because God starts to communicate himself as he is and not as we would imagine him. When this profound prayer becomes experiential the believer begins to experience the love of God as never before.

The only hope that any human being has of being changed permanently for the better is in and through a relationship where love is freely given and returned in kind. That hope is given to you in the mutual love that binds you and Pat together and overflows on to your children. That's why marriage is a sacrament, because it replicates in human terms the loving that binds the Father to the Son for eternity. That hope – of permanent change for the better – is not however given to those who accept a life of perpetual chastity but who are, for whatever reason, denied the direct experience of God's love. To deny those who make such a choice the experience of God's love through prayer is not only to condemn them to a heartless life, but to place them in what the old text books would call a serious occasion of sin.

This matter is important – not just to help us understand why, thanks to the aftermath of Quietism, so many have left, but to see how renewal must come about and how your contribution as a mother is vital to it. That's why I must return to this matter again in my next letter; for now that will have to suffice.

Love
David

17

Training for Chastity

Dear Susanna,
I in no way meant to surprise or shock you, I just wanted you to know the truth. Endless pretence and cover-ups will only put off renewal and lead to more and more young people wasting years of their lives joining institutions that often prevent them from realising the ideals that led them there in the first place.

Way back in the seventies, I spoke at a seminar for Franciscans which had been set up to try to discover why so many of their number had left in recent years. The main speaker was a psychologist who, competent and entertaining as he was in his own field, didn't know much about religious life or what was needed to reinvigorate it. In a long conversation amongst a group of friars one of them said that in the seven years of his training he hadn't had a single talk on prayer, and the others all agreed with him. I was writing a book on prayer at the time so I made contact with other religious orders belonging to the older apostolic tradition, only to find that the experience of their members barely differed. Some admitted to having been given a few talks on the rudimentaries, but none had received any talks or lectures about the profound contemplative prayer that was once thought to be their *raison d'être.*

When the first apostolic orders were founded in the thirteenth century St Thomas Aquinas coined a phrase that they all accepted as summing up their calling. It was this: 'Contemplare contemplari aliis trahere'. In simple English it means that their job was first to contemplate and then to share the fruits of contemplation with others. It was precisely because they did this that the orders grew rapidly and transformed Christendom, much of which had fallen not just into religious laxity or apathy, but into a virulent form of neo-paganism. St Thomas insisted that, 'Nemo enim dat quod non habat'. In other words, you can only communicate to others what you yourself have received. It should be common-sense Christianity, but it had been forgotten at the time, as it has been today. In short, Jesus was himself the most mature and stable human being because he not only knew with his mind that he was loved, but he tangibly experienced that love progressively penetrating and permeating his whole being. That's why he spoke with power and authority and had such a profound effect on all who heard him, promising that it would be the same for those who would follow him.

Long before St Thomas used the word 'contemplation' it had been used to describe the experience of this same divine life that progressively penetrated Jesus as it did those who chose to follow him. It was called mystical or hidden because it was hidden from all but those who experienced it, bringing about the 'hidden plan of God' within them so that they, like Jesus himself, would then be empowered to communicate it to others. The older apostolic orders (nor any other orders or congregations for that matter) will not renew themselves by turning to psychology to do it for them, but by returning to their own sources and the evangelical tradition on which they were based.

If a priest or a religious is, for whatever reason, deprived of regular access to the experience of this supernatural love, while at the same time being denied natural love, disaster is bound to follow. Then, when the media gloats over these incidents, and interviews rectors and spiritual directors of seminaries or novice masters or mistresses, to put them on the spot, we are sadly treated to vague generalisations under the heading of 'training for chastity'. It is assumed that there is some such training that can prepare a person to forgo what their bodies, quite naturally and understandably, pine for and that this will prevent these regrettable failures in the future. We are deceiving ourselves if we think that anything other than guiding a person to the contemplative experience of God's love will help them. Only this will satisfy, sustain and maintain their human and spiritual well-being. Anything short of this will lead to failure.

When this profound prayer becomes part of their life, those praying will begin to experience the love of God as never before. As this experience of being loved gradually transforms them it will enable them to communicate the love of God to others, not just because they have heard about it or read about it, but because they have experienced it for themselves and that makes all the difference.

This is why great saints, like St Francis of Assisi, St Dominic, St Catherine and St Bernadine of Siena and St Vincent Ferrier, converted hundreds of thousands through their preaching. When they spoke, it was clear that the same Spirit who was present in Jesus spoke through them and entered into those who heard them. Only apostles such as these can bring about the renewal we are still waiting for.

Love,
David

18

Celibacy and Service

Dear Susanna,

I believe you. I have no doubt that your parish priest is a good man. I could say the same for my own parish priest, and in particular the priest who has inspired me more than any other has. However, he assured me that it was not because of, but in spite of, the limited spiritual training he received in the seminary, that he discovered for himself the contemplative prayer that he was able to teach me. Many of the good priests on whom we depend for spiritual guidance could say 'amen' to that.

It was exactly the same for those who became saints, since the anti-mystical witch hunts did so much damage to Christian spirituality. These people became as they were despite an imbalance that made the contemplative prayer available to only a few. The majority had to seek the knowledge they needed for themselves and usually against heavy odds. You can read their stories for yourself, from St John of the Cross to Padre Pio. Read how they suffered from the spiritual ignoramuses who were their superiors and their spiritual directors, who more often than not misguided them. St Teresa of Avila often complained about the quality of her own spiritual directors, who wasted so much of her time leading her into one cul-de-sac after another.

Yes, I do believe in chastity for all religious and all priests who freely embrace it. Nevertheless, I believe it is not only valueless but also wrong to allow or insist that a person should make such a vow unless they are at the same time given genuine training for chastity – that is, proper preparation for contemplation. If, for whatever reason, a person cannot be led to this experience, I believe it is wrong for them to make a vow or promise of chastity, as a necessary condition of serving the community as a priest.

In the Early Church there were two distinct groups serving the faithful in different ways. The first group was known as the 'virgines et continentes'. They lived in their own homes, or later in communities, taking vows of chastity or the equivalent in those days. Almost all the early fathers wrote special treatises for them, called 'ad virgines', to help support and encourage them. Without exception the fathers insisted that if they didn't plunge themselves into a prayer life that led to the experience of God's action within, then the life of virginity would lead to spiritual barrenness and then to disaster. However, no such treatises were written for 'priests' because most were married and called not to a particular way of life but to a particular form of liturgical service. If, in subsequent centuries, the Church insisted that chastity should become obligatory for priests, for what were seen as 'good and practical reasons' at the time, then for 'good and practical reasons' at a later time that law could be repealed. I believe such reasons exist today.

After chastity became obligatory, spiritual writers began to write for priests, offering the same sort of advice that had been given earlier to the 'virgines et continentes': namely, that unless chastity be complemented by contemplation it would lead to disaster since 'no man can live without pleasure', as St Thomas Aquinas put it. Therefore, if a priest does not have pleasure out of the mystical encounter with God he'll begin to search for it elsewhere. No one, therefore, should be asked to promise chastity without at the same time being shown how to complement it with the experience of divine love. I could go further and say it would be morally wrong to ask someone to do this just so that they can be more available to serve the Church and be more pliable in the hands of their superiors. It would, as we have seen in recent years, lead to serious moral lapses. However, what we have not seen is the devastating effect it can have on the lives of those who escape the eye of the media, but who suffer loveless, lonely lives that inevitably diminish the example and the service they should be giving to others. A life of perpetual chastity is a very high ideal and a special calling for the few. However, the faithful should not be deprived of ready access to the sacraments, whose strength they need, just because those who do not feel called to embrace chastity are prevented from serving them as priests.

Those who freely choose to embrace chastity do so in a spirit of trust, believing and expecting that those who are responsible for their training will guide them by their example and direction to the love for which they have given up so much. This responsibility falls first on bishops and provincials, then on rectors of seminaries and those responsible for formation. Woe betide those who fail them.

Love,

David

19

A Message for a PP

Dear Susanna,
I'm afraid your friend is wrong. The fact that he's got a busy parish to run doesn't mean he should pray less, it means he should pray more. St Francis de Sales used to say that you should have at least half an hour for personal prayer each day, unless of course you're very busy. Then you should have at least an hour! Your friend is also wrong when he says that contemplative prayer is for contemplative monks. The Christian tradition is quite clear that the more time you have to spend working in the world the more time you need for personal prayer.

Some years ago I went on a retreat given by Cardinal Hume. He quoted from the rule of St Benedict that stated, 'If you would pray privately make it swift and ardent'. He then explained how prolonged time for personal prayer is not so important in the monastic ideal when public and private prayer become as one in the solemn liturgical celebration of the divine office. This prayer is nourished by slow, meditative readings from the scriptures till it overflows into the rest of one's monastic life and work. For this to work properly the halcyon seclusion of a monastery is needed. This is how the monk attains 'the prayer without ceasing' when every moment is a moment for gently trying to raise the heart and mind to God. The Cardinal explained how his new job entailed learning a different approach to prayer that could no longer depend on the support of his fellow monks in the monastic choir or workplace. He walked over to a group of Franciscan friars and said, 'I have to learn from these men and their tradition.' In other words, he had to be busy in the same world that they inhabited, fulfilling his apostolate as the Archbishop of the largest diocese in England. He had to learn to turn more to the personal, private prayer, that did not have the same importance in his monastic seclusion, not only in his new cathedral home, but on the plane, the underground or in a taxi as he travelled alone to fulfil his new commitments.

He saw quite clearly why the genius of St Francis emphasised the importance of personal, private prayer as a way to the prayer of contemplation. This would enable him to achieve 'the prayer without ceasing' throughout his travels, his preaching and the service of the lepers and other social outcasts whom he had been called to serve.

All the other mendicant orders followed suit in their own way and according to their traditions; that's why they were initially so successful. Contrary to popular belief, personal prayer as a means to contemplation came back into Christian spirituality with a renewed urgency with the mendicants, not the monks. More than eighty per cent of the great mystical writers, from St Francis to St John of the Cross, were mendicants, not monks. It was they who, like the Cardinal, realised that contemplative prayer not only sustains the busy apostle, but enables the prayer that is first learnt and practised at set periods of the day, to overflow and envelop every moment of the day. Contemplation, not meditation, is the perfect prayer for someone busily trying to live out their Christian life in the world. You can't recite prayers or meditate easily while you are working or travelling, but you can contemplate, because contemplation does not depend on words, images or reasoning, but on the same experience of the presence of

God that Jesus continually felt throughout his life and work on earth. That's why it's important to pass through and beyond meditation as soon as possible, but sadly there are so few teachers today who know the way.

Please tell your friend that his patron saint the Curé d'Ars transformed a non-practising, half-pagan parish not by the latest theological fashions, that only pay lip service to prayer, nor by surrounding himself with the latest computer technology, but by spending hours on his knees. As the Holy Spirit changed him it changed others through him, not just his own parishioners, but the forty thousand people a week who flocked to hear him preach in his remote little parish. When the friars go back to relearn the spiritual tradition from their founders, and parish priests relearn theirs from their patron saint and teach their students and seminarians to do likewise, then renewal will have begun.

I sincerely hope I'm wrong but I think that seminaries, student houses and houses of formation still place all the practical emphasis on academic knowledge whilst preparation for contemplation comes a poor second, if it comes anywhere in the official programme. What we need in the Church above all else is the leadership of priests and religious who are taught first how to receive and experience the wisdom that comes through deep contemplative prayer, and secondly the knowledge that comes through books. Then the renewal we are still waiting for will have begun in earnest and not before time!

Love,
David

20

Back to Contemplation

Dear Susanna,

Contemplation is the word used to describe the experience of the action of the Holy Spirit within. It was the continual experience of Jesus throughout his life on earth and the source from which he drew his strength. For those who would follow him this experience usually starts after they have passed through what's called 'first fervour' and after an initial purification that can go on for months or even years. It is characterised by dryness and aridity, an inability to pray as before, though the desire for God still remains and even becomes stronger. I explained all these signs in my book *The Mystic* so I won't do so again. In time – of God's choosing, not ours – a person begins to experience the action of the Holy Spirit within. The Spirit is both love and truth at one and the same time, so anyone who perseveres will begin to experience the love of God to various degrees of intensity. Over years rather than months this experience begins to seep out of the set times for prayer to encompass the whole day. This gives a priest or religious the help, the strength, the inner resources and the consolation that they might have otherwise received indirectly through a husband or wife and the children who embody their love.

Now, when many of the young priests and religious who were filled with enthusiasm to convey the teachings of Vatican II had their wings clipped by their seniors, few had the inner resources needed to battle on indefinitely. Their own human enthusiasm alone could not sustain them for ever without some sort of support, so frustration and depression over their predicament led to the biggest walk-out the Church has ever known. Many sought what they had originally hoped to find within, in the sacrament of love, but even this was denied the majority of them. They felt understandably aggrieved that they were expected to live in a 'loveless limbo-land' by the same institution that denied them the love for which they believed they'd been called.

Although I'm not pointing the finger at individuals, but rather at a set of unfortunate historical circumstances for this sad state of affairs, something must nevertheless be done and done quickly or the haemorrhage will continue. Seminaries and houses of formation must surround the young with teachers who are above all else men and women of prayer, who are known to pray daily and in whom the fruits of contemplation are there for all to see. Almost anyone can help beginners, but these teachers must have learnt of the purification that precedes contemplation by their own experience. If such people cannot be found within the formation team then spiritual directors must be brought in from outside to save these beginners from spiritual disaster later.

I'm not suggesting that those who do not receive this help will all leave at a later stage – this is not necessarily true. Like many who preceded them, they may remain but seek what they failed to find in the spiritual life in substitutes that will never satisfy, and may even destroy them. They'll begin to make a career of their calling, seeking positions of power and prestige, assuaging the emptiness within with over-indulgence in food and drink or in illicit sexual substitutes. This may ruin not only their lives but the lives of those whom they had originally come to serve.

No, I don't agree with that priest you spoke to. It's nonsense to argue that this emphasis on contemplation would lead to a decline in academic standards, when exactly the reverse would take place. The Holy Spirit is both love and truth so his action will transform not only the heart but also the mind, giving the wisdom that Jesus promised at the Last Supper. This will enable contemplative students to understand their theological studies far more deeply than the students who depend on purely academic knowledge, no matter how intelligent they may be. These are the leaders we need in the Church today, not priests and religious who are well versed only in academic knowledge, but those who are also full of the love and wisdom that they can share with those who turn to them.

I have the distinct impression that despite the great losses sustained since Vatican II and the ensuing decline in standards in the priesthood and the religious life, little if anything is being done about this in seminaries and houses of formation. I would be delighted if letters came pouring in from students and teachers alike to correct me. I would be glad to be told that priorities have at last changed, and the priests and religious we need so badly are at last getting the spiritual training that we also need to receive through them. It would be a delight because at last it would be evident that lessons had been learnt from the past, and that the profound contemplative reformers, who changed the Church in the past, were being prepared to do the same in the immediate future.

Love,
David

21

Boys Will Be Boys

Dear Susanna,
I thought that mothers with four young children were supposed to stay at home and vegetate instead of thinking up difficult theological questions to tie me in knots! No sooner do I answer one set of questions than you think of some more; this time it's a set of thorny theological ones! I can't answer them all in this letter because it will take all my time to answer the first: 'Why did the twelve-year-old Jesus put his parents through such agony while he was astounding the temple teachers?'

The reason why this story from the gospels has puzzled you is because you were brought up in the 'old theology' and this, with all its own shortcomings, was further distorted by an old heresy. As I try to explain what I mean by this I hope you will be able to see how what I've called the 'new theology' will help to explain it. It will answer your question more accurately because it sticks closer to the scriptures by turning to the divinely inspired theology of the authors of the New Testament. I will follow the same approach in answering your other questions later, but to start with let me deal with your first question.

If I were to stick to the letter of the 'old theology', distorted by an old heresy, I would find myself caught on the horns of a dilemma. You see, if Jesus was God, and therefore knew everything, then why didn't he know what he was putting his parents through? If he didn't know, how could he be God, who would of course know everything? The traditional way out of the dilemma is to admit that as God he did know everything, but 'being busy about his father's business' outweighed putting his parents through a living nightmare. Not the sort of loving, caring God that Jesus described later!

There isn't really a dilemma at all, except the dilemma made by the rather impoverished idea we have of the Incarnation – thanks to a third-century heretic called Arius. He stated quite explicitly that 'though Christ was a great man, even the greatest man who ever lived, he wasn't God'.

Although you might not have heard of Arianism, it is arguably the most pernicious heresy the Church has ever known. At the time the vast majority of Christians were converted to it. Now this is a good example of how Greek philosophy, with its subtle and precise language, can be so useful. Without it the early fathers of the Church would have had great difficulty in defending orthodoxy. However, it will also enable me to show how in defending the faith so vigorously, a distortion can take place that sullies the purity of the simple message of the gospel. Although subtle theological arguments might have carried weight with the intelligentsia, another tack had to be taken for ordinary people who couldn't follow these arguments. For them the teaching of the gospel was only maintained by the continual repetition of the slogan 'Christ is God', over and over again. This helped to keep those who couldn't follow complex theological arguments on the straight and narrow. It succeeded so well that in the centuries that followed even some of the more important Christian writers used the word Christ to mean God, and God for Christ, indiscriminately. They didn't feel the need or see the importance of distinguishing one from the other.

Every victory, of course, is won at a price, and the price of the Church's victory over Arianism was to undermine the importance and the meaning of the Incarnation, not just at the time, but right down to the present day. Hence your question which demonstrates how you, with all too many others, have imbibed a Catholic education that is still affected by the aftermath of a heresy that is over fifteen hundred years old. Let me explain a little more clearly what I mean. When God freely chose to enter into our human nature he wasn't play-acting, it was for real. You see when God chooses to do something, he doesn't do it by halves, he does it perfectly. When he freely chose to become a human baby it actually involved experiencing the same limitations as your babies, because that's what he wanted. As he grew into boyhood he had to learn everything, from how to play to how to dress himself. When he was enjoying himself or absorbed in something that really interested him he might forget to come home for tea, as your boys sometimes do. This is not sinful, but the sort of forgetfulness that all boys experience. I know, three days is a long time, but he was a boy genius totally absorbed in his favourite subject, and who's to say that he knew his parents had actually left for home anyway. After all, if for whatever reason it took them three days to realise that he hadn't come with them, then the same reason could explain why three days could pass before he realised they'd gone without him.

Afterwards, on reflection, he would be sorry for how he'd behaved, and would say so like any well-brought-up boy, and so learn to avoid making the same mistake again. This is clearly implied by St Luke who said that after this incident he went down to Nazareth with his parents 'where he lived under their authority' (2:51). That he continued to grow not just in physical but psychological stature is not just implied but clearly stated by St Luke on two distinct occasions. At the same time he made it clear that this human growth was complemented by a corresponding spiritual development through which he grew 'in wisdom and understanding with the years', and in an ever-deepening relationship with his Father (2:52 and 2:40).

The more clearly we understand precisely what it meant for Christ to enter into our weak human nature then the better we will be able to see why he chose to do it, and the profound implications this has for our personal spiritual lives. When I was a student during the time before the Council this sort of theological reasoning was thought to be heretical. But, as I hope you can see, it is in fact the teaching of the divinely inspired theology of St Luke – and the other Evangelists for that matter! I hope all this makes sense. I'll explain more next time.

Love,
David

22

The Hour-glass

Dear Susanna,
You are right – that's exactly what I was trying to say. The Word was not just made flesh, but made baby too, made boy, made adolescent, and made man, until he was transformed by the Spirit, so that others could be transformed too.

The holiest man I've ever met explained how this transformation took place in Jesus, and how it can take place in us also, in a unique way that I have never forgotten. Fr Macarius had been living as a monk at a remote monastery in Africa for over fifty years. He took what I thought to be an over-sized egg-timer and put it on the table in front of me. It was in fact an hour-glass, still used to measure the time given to personal prayer in the monastery. He turned it upside-down on the table, explaining that the top half of the hour-glass, filled with sand, represented the divine nature of Jesus that was his from the moment 'the Word was made flesh'. The empty half represented the human nature that he chose to enter simultaneously, not just to share in and experience our human weakness, but to use as a means of communicating to others the same Holy Spirit that gradually filled and then transformed him. The sand represented the Holy Spirit. As I watched the hour-glass slowly emptying in front of me, Fr Macarius explained that as Jesus grew physically, psychologically and spiritually his human nature was progressively filled by the Holy Spirit that he was constantly open to receive. However, the father went on to explain that, if the analogy were perfect, the top half of the hour-glass would never empty because infinite love is inexhaustible.

He then said that, as Jesus grew 'in wisdom and understanding with the years', his weak human nature became more and more perfect as it was suffused by the divine. When it was filled to overflowing with the same Spirit, that had first conceived and then completed him, Jesus' human nature became a prism – not a lifeless prism made of glass or quartz, but of human flesh and blood permeated through and through by the divine. This human prism could transmit to other human beings the self-same Spirit that had already transformed him: a single glance, a loving touch or a few heart-felt words were all that was necessary.

But Jesus was still limited, because although his human nature had become a prism, the same laws of space and time that confined everyone else restricted him too. They limited the number of people who could approach him at any given time. Meeting him would always be a matter of coming and going, it could never be permanent. That's why he made it plain that he would have to leave all the limitations of this world, where the 'Word' had first been made flesh, to go to another place. Here there would be no restrictions that could prevent him from reaching everyone instead of just a few. It was from here that his transformed and transfigured human body became a timeless prism that enabled the divine to reach out through him to all men and women of every time and every place simultaneously.

When Jesus realised that his days were numbered he prepared his followers to accept a new way that he had devised so that he could remain with them to the end of time. As a human being himself he knew that this means would have to be seeable, touchable, and even consumable, to have the desired effect. The most readily available food at the time would be transformed in such a way that it could sustain his active presence not just amongst them, but within them. This would enable him to enter into them and then overflow continually from within into anyone who admitted him, with the same Spirit that had progressively filled his own human nature, throughout his life on earth.

Fr Macarius first learnt the practical significance of these profound truths from his novice master. His teacher told him that although Jesus had chosen to enter into him through the mysteries of the bread and wine, that presence would have little or no effect if he didn't remain open to receive, digest and assimilate what was given, through prayer. Whenever the novices gathered for prayer the hour-glass was placed in front of them, not just to measure the time they prayed, but to remind them all of how they could be transformed too by the same Spirit who transformed Jesus.

When I returned from my travels I toured the local antique shops to find an hour-glass of my own. It has reminded me ever since of all I learnt from Fr Macarius. I know you haven't got one, but what about that egg-timer that hangs above your kitchen sink? It might be small, but it can help you understand the biggest mystery of our faith!

Love,
David

23

Food for Love

Dear Susanna,

I know exactly what you mean. We had someone in my parish just like that, only in this case it was an old man. He never missed any weekday Mass. Not only that, if there were any other Masses going that day he'd be there. Yet just like the 'pious old woman' you describe, he was one of the bitterest people I've ever met.

Of course this doesn't mean that the Mass is ineffectual in itself, it just means that it has failed to have an effect on these people. Merely being present at a Mass doesn't change anyone; it's not a magic rite that automatically transforms anyone who attends it. If this were the case then every priest and every religious would be walking saints with haloes round their heads and lilies in their hands. But this is patently not the case.

If there is nothing wrong with the Mass then there must be something wrong with those people who regularly attend or 'say' it yet remain no better, if no worse, than anyone else. You see, in a single Mass more energy is released than is contained in the whole universe many times over, but this energy is unleashed in the form of love. Contrary to any other form of energy, however, love can't be forced on anyone who doesn't freely choose to receive it. That's the very nature of love; forced love is simply a contradiction in terms. It takes serious preparation, then, to receive this power of love that can change us permanently for the better.

Yet time and time again we rush into Mass at the last minute with precious little time to put our thoughts together, never mind taking time for the serious preparation that's needed for the most important event in our lives. Then, all too often, the moment the Mass ends we are off chattering with friends as we dash home for Sunday dinner. Little thought is given to the awesome event in which we have just taken part, nor do we give ourselves time to assimilate and digest what has been received. If only we gave the same time we know we need to enjoy and digest our Sunday meal to this sacred meal then the same love that transformed Jesus would be well on the way to transforming us too.

Before Jesus, people believed that their lives could be changed by merely being present at mystic rites and ceremonies so long as they observed all the rules and practices of ritual purity demanded by the law. In other words, they believed in magic. Sadly, two thousand years on, all too many people still believe in magic – they still believe that their mere presence at Mass is enough. It might be enough to assuage their guilt, or pay the premium on the spiritual insurance they feel they need, but it will never change them no matter how many Masses they attend.

When Jesus came it was to proclaim a 'New World Order' in which people could only be changed by love, never by magic. Although this love is embodied in a unique way in the Sacred Mysteries it is in fact being poured out all the time. But before we can be open to receive it at all times we need to learn how to receive it at set times when its presence can be seen, touched, and even digested to help our fragile faith. That's why Jesus provided for such an eventuality on the night before he died, at the most sacred meal ever celebrated.

Now we can appreciate better why the word 'gospel' means 'good news'. It is simply because it's the best news the world has ever heard. First, because it is the story of how 'uncreated love' not only enters into created time and space, but into human flesh and blood, and thence into ordinary food and drink to transform all who receive it. Secondly, it describes precisely what Jesus had to do in order to prepare himself to receive that love into his own human nature, so that we can learn from his example how to receive it into ours. So the burning question is: what precisely did he have to do to facilitate the transformation of his own life by the Holy Spirit and then transform ours in the same way? When we know the answer to this we will know the secret of the spiritual life, for then we will know not only how to receive the love that's poured out each time we go to Mass, but how to receive the same love that is all around us, if we only knew it! But that answer is too important to give in the short time that's left to me now, so it will have to wait until next time.

Love,
David

24

Returning Home

Dear Susanna,
I am so sorry, I didn't mean to keep you in suspense. The reason why I didn't want to explain last time how Jesus received the love that transformed him was because without a full explanation I could easily have shocked you. You might have stopped writing to me and written me off as a heretic! Now I may say things in strange or unusual ways from time to time, but believe me, this journalist's not for burning. Well, I suppose that's for you to say. But please hear me out before you condemn me to the stake. Are you ready?

This, then, is what Jesus had to do – he had to repent! Well, don't say I didn't warn you! The reason why you are surprised, if not shocked, is because you, like the rest of the 'human rat race', are a sinner. Sinners only understand repentance in one way. It means to turn back to God after committing sin, and they usually associate it with feelings of guilt and remorse. However, the meaning of repentance is far wider than that. It means to turn back to God from everything that would turn our attention elsewhere – from temptation, for instance. The scriptures make it quite plain that Jesus 'was tempted in all things, as we are tempted' (Hebrews 4:15). However, unlike us, he never gave in. So what must he have done? He must have turned away from it and turned his full attention back to God; in other words, he repented.

If you read the gospels you will see Jesus encountering many temptations, but you'll also see that he never gives in to any of them. Look at him, for instance, praying in the desert. There he was tempted time and time again but he never gave in. In other words, he kept turning away from those temptations and kept turning back to God to receive in ever greater measure the help and strength he needed for what lay before him.

Throughout the rest of his time on earth he was relentlessly tempted, as you can read for yourself, but he never falls. Only hours before he was brutally done to death you can see him in the Garden of Gethsemane struggling with the terrible temptation to seek an easier way than the one before him, but he never gave in. He kept turning back to his Father for the help and strength he needed to do his Father's will and to do it to the bitter end. Even when he was dying in agony he was tempted yet again, this time to come down from the cross to prove who he really was and to demonstrate the powers that he claimed he had been given. Once again he resisted that temptation and died carrying out and recommitting himself to his Father's will. In other words, unlike all too many other preachers, he first practised himself what he then preached to others. That's why so many people responded to his call for repentance, to enable the Holy Spirit to work in them as it had in him.

An old Chinese sage was once asked, 'If you could do one thing to change the world what would it be?' He replied without hesitation, 'I would give back to words their original meaning!' If we can only dust the cobwebs off the word 'repentance' and see it again in its original meaning then it will enable us to understand anew the response that will enable God to transform us.

Forget the Greek word *metanoia*; Jesus didn't preach in Greek but in Aramaic, a language with its roots in Hebrew,

and here the true meaning of 'repentance' can be found in the word *shub.* It means 'to return', more precisely 'to return home'. The prophets used the word to tell people to return to God – to return to their true home. Isaiah used the word to describe the return of sons to the father they had rejected, and Jesus followed suit. But he gave it a new meaning that shocked his contemporaries when he said that the one to whom you must return is not just your Father but your Dad (Abba). The word 'father' can have different meanings in any language, but the word 'daddy' almost always means a parent who gives the life and love that everyone needs. This love is vital if we are to grow into the sort of whole and mature people we would all like to become. If this is what human love can do for us how much more can 'Our Dad who art in heaven' do for those who freely choose to return home and to remain at all times open to his love? Next time I write I'll tell you more about what we can do to enable our 'ever-loving Dad' to change our lives permanently for the better.
Love,
David

25

Responding in Kind

Dear Susanna,
You're right – the story of the prodigal son does sum up much of what I've been trying to say. In the most human and the most captivating parable of all, God is presented as the 'ever-loving Dad', whose forgiveness for the wayward son who returns home knows no bounds. Nevertheless, it doesn't say everything about repentance. In the scriptures there's no word for a person, or a group of persons, who have repented, but only for those who are in the process of repenting – continually trying to return home. You see, as long as we remain human we'll need to repent time and time again until we return home for good. Even though the prodigal returns home don't think he will never fail his father again, because he will, even though he may never seriously turn his back on him as he did before.

The spiritual life is nothing other than the journey of a person who continually chooses to get up after having fallen, to turn back to God, knowing that their 'ever-loving Dad' will never fail them. Stop and think about it for a moment or two and you'll see that the word 'repentance' is merely the word the Bible uses to sum up what is involved in returning love in kind.

Seen in this light it involves four inseparable ingredients. First, it involves turning or, more precisely, continually turning back to the One whose love never fails as ours does. Secondly, it involves being open and remaining open as long as our human frailty permits us to receive and experience the only love that can change us permanently.

Thirdly, it involves emptying and purifying. The more we allow 'pure love' to draw closer to us, the more it highlights the impurity of our own love that has to be purified before the union that we all desire can take place. Anyone who has experienced being loved knows how unworthy they feel when he or she experiences the selfless love of another reaching out to them. It not only makes a person want to change to be worthy of what they receive, but it also gives them the strength to bring about the desired change. Great mystical writers like St John of the Cross describe how divine love purifies a person to prepare them for what they desire more than anything else. God is pure, unadulterated selflessness. We are impure, adulterated selfishness. Before union can be brought about a certain likeness has to be found. St Irenaeus said that God created us in his own image, then the Holy Spirit was sent to create us in his likeness. Continually turning and opening to God enables the Holy Spirit to enter us and re-create us in his likeness. That's what happens to the spiritual travellers who continually turn and open themselves to the fire of the Holy Spirit, enabling him to purify them of all dross so that gold can be united to gold.

The fourth ingredient is surrender. As we are purified, so is our imperfect human loving, enabling us to be fitted ever more perfectly into Christ, in and through whom we can continually surrender ourselves to God, knowing that our offering will be accepted.

This whole process is seen to best advantage when a Christian community comes together to return love in kind at the sacred sacrificial meal that is at the heart of our faith. However, the quality of our giving at this sacred celebration will be determined by the giving that has already taken place through the personal repentance that precedes it. In other words, the Mass is not magic, and so the profound effect that it can have on our lives will be determined by the quality of the selfless loving that we practise. This loving is learnt through repeated repentance.

Prayer is the word used to describe the act where loving is learnt through continually practising repentance. If this doesn't make sense, then just try to pray regularly for any length of time and you'll find yourself endlessly trying to turn away from distractions and to turn back to God. If you have fifty distractions in five minutes it means you've practised repentance fifty times through prayer. It means you've acted selflessly fifty times too, and taken the first steps in learning a habit of loving that will enable you to love others more perfectly outside of prayer. In the same way the selfless giving that you have practised both inside and outside of prayer will enable you to love God more perfectly inside the Mass, where we always receive to the measure of our giving.

Perhaps all this will become clearer if I can explain in a little more detail exactly what happens, or what should happen, when we come together to share in the same sacred meal that Jesus celebrated with his disciples on the night before he died. I will try to do that in my next letter.

Love,
David

26

At-one-ment

Dear Susanna,
In order to explain as clearly as I can what happens at Mass I want you to picture in your imagination an Old Testament sacrifice. Imagine a shepherd called James choosing a lamb and sacrificing it to God. When the lamb is burnt on the altar of sacrifice the smoke and the flames rise heavenwards. If his sacrifice was offered with 'a humble and contrite heart' it would be accepted. Then God would send his Holy Spirit who would mysteriously descend through the smoke and fire to penetrate and possess the lamb. What had been James' lamb now becomes God's Lamb. So when James and his family took and ate what became known as 'The Lamb of God' they were all drawn into a profound union with God himself and with one another through the sacred meal, without which the sacrifice would be incomplete.

When John the Baptist pointed to Jesus and said, 'Look, there is the Lamb of God' (John 1:30), everybody knew exactly what he meant. Consequently, when Jesus said that whosoever eats his flesh and drinks his blood would receive the same life with which God had penetrated him, his listeners understood quite well what he was saying, even though it might have shocked them into disbelief.

Now, for a Jew of that period, the word 'flesh' didn't mean what we would call meat, nor did 'blood' just mean the red liquid that flows out of it. They meant the whole person. When, therefore, Jesus invited people to eat his 'flesh' and drink his 'blood' the invitation was to receive him into themselves – 'Body, blood, soul and divinity' – so that they could have communion with him. Then, through him, they could enter into a deep mystical union or 'at-one-ment' with God, and with each other. This is why he was and still is called 'The Lamb of God, who takes away the sin of the world', because the Holy Spirit who draws people into him, simultaneously purifies them of all that separates them from God and from one another.

However, the new meaning and significance that Jesus gave to this profound union can only be fully appreciated by realising precisely what happened at the Last Supper. You see, when ordinary bread and wine were changed they did not become so much 'The Lamb of God' who preached to the people of Palestine but rather 'The Lamb of God' who rose from the dead on the first Easter Day. They became 'The Lamb of God' who was radioactive with the fullness of God's life that completely transformed and transfigured him into a new and glorified human being. So whoever receives this sacred bread and wine is led into a close personal communion with the Risen One himself.

The ultimate meaning of this 'Holy Communion' can only be fully appreciated when we realise that it leads a person, not just to share in the life of 'The Risen Lord', but to be part of his very action, his pure and perfect love of his Father. In other words, they are drawn up into the vortex of life and love that endlessly reaches out from him into God, to be returned in kind for all eternity. It is into this Trinity of everlasting life and love that Jesus came to invite us.

My favourite icon, that always hangs in our dining room, is Andrei Rublev's mysterious and mystical masterpiece that depicts this awesome invitation. It also helps to remind us of the profound communion into which we are called each time we go to Mass, and of the pure and contrite heart that will alone enable us to participate in it, as we should. Most important of all, it's to remind us of the loving learnt in prayer and practised through love of neighbour, which is the offering that we make in union with the offering of Jesus. If we haven't practised any loving since we last came to Mass then we have nothing to offer, and if we have nothing to offer then what do we expect to receive?

Once again, the Mass is not magic. Even the most powerful energy in heaven and on earth can have no effect on the person who has made no attempt to practise the loving that alone can open them to 'The Fountain of Love', no matter how many times they go to Mass. A person can only receive to the measure of their giving.

The Mass is called a sacrifice, because it is the time and place where our self-sacrificial loving is united with Christ's, to be offered to the Father in, with and through him, ensuring that it will always be received. However, this sacrifice should always be completed by the sacred meal in which we receive the very life and love of God himself through the bread and wine that is permeated by his presence. That's why the word 'sacrifice' is made up of two Latin words that mean 'to make holy'. But yet again we must remember that we only receive from this sacred meal to the measure in which we have already given.

Love,
David

27

The Mystic at Mass

Dear Susanna,
Sometimes I think my letters are beginning to sound like extracts from a theology textbook. So let me give you a practical example of what I've been trying to say by showing you how the greatest mystic of all prepared to take part in the Mass, and then assimilated what he had received.

The mystic is Jesus Christ himself. He made it clear that he had come to do not his own will but the will of his Father. Now, what his Father wanted him to do was what he wants us to do too – namely, to love God with our whole minds and hearts and with our whole strength, and to love our neighbour as ourselves. Jesus spent his whole life doing this in spite of strong temptations to do otherwise. As a result, when he offered up a life of unremitting selflessness and self-giving at the Last Supper he was able to receive in return the love of God to the measure of his giving.

However, although Jesus was able to receive what was given in an unprecedented way, he was still a human being. This meant that he needed time to digest, assimilate and personalise the love of his Father more fully in prayer, just like other human beings. That's why he needed to go into the Garden of Gethsemane to pray. As he prayed, hour after hour, he was caught up in a battle with the powers of evil that relentlessly tried to divert him from his purpose. It was while he was in the act of turning away from temptation and opening himself to God that the love transmitted in the sacrament he'd just received penetrated him more and more fully, giving him the help and strength he needed. This enabled him to make yet again the same self-sacrifice that he'd been making throughout his life, but this time through torture, crucifixion and death the following day.

The apostles were only beginners. They'd not given much yet, so they couldn't receive much either. That's why they couldn't pray for long, that's why they ran away when the trouble started, and that's why Peter betrayed Jesus. Their time would come after many years of self-giving and self-sacrifice. Then they too would be able to participate fully in the 'breaking of the bread' as Jesus had done. Then their self-sacrifice would enable them to receive the love that would give them the power to do what Jesus had done, and do it to the bitter end.

We too are beginners in the spiritual life, like those first apostles before the resurrection. Like them we've got to learn from the man whose example we are all called to follow. What we've got to learn is how to give, first to God, and then to our neighbours, all the love we can muster in the currency of self-sacrificial service. This is the offering that we are then asked to make when we come to Mass. It is always accepted too, because it's offered, not just alongside, but in, with and through Christ himself.

When God offers us in return the same love that Jesus received at the Last Supper, we must receive it in exactly the same way as he did. In other words, time must be allowed after the offering we've made at Mass to digest, assimilate and personalise what we've received at the holiest communion imaginable. If the responsibility of feeding our families prevents us from doing this immediately it must be done later, preferably on the same day, because that's what Sunday is supposed to be for and that's how we make it holy.

This love must be received through the same sort of prayer that Jesus practised in Gethsemane. It is imperative to understand that the endless battle against distractions and temptation that we all experience in prayer, far from being a waste of time, is the best possible use of time. After all, what better use of time can there possibly be than practising the selfless loving that makes human beings lovable? That's what prayer is for, and that's why God is the first to love us in return as we try to love him. Then the love received enables us to leave the training ground, empowered to love God ever more perfectly, but this time through the neighbour in need with whom he identifies himself.

Through the Mass, then, we are drawn up into a mysterious cycle of giving and receiving, of dying and being reborn, that enables the believer to enter more and more fully, not just into Christ's life, but into his action. As this mysterious cycle recurs throughout each successive liturgical year we are progressively fitted into Christ, until, like St Paul, we can say, 'It is no longer I who live but Christ who lives in me' (Galatians 2:20).

As you can see, I have enclosed a recent tape I made – 'The Prayer of Christ' – that explains what I've been trying to say in greater detail. Let me know what you think about it.

Love,
David

28

Liturgical Love

Dear Susanna,
Sometimes I dream of writing a book to explain Christianity for complete outsiders. I'd like to write it without using any of the traditional jargon that can be such a stumbling-block to understanding a message that's meant to be for all. It would help insiders too, like yourself, who have been brought up on religious terminology that's never been properly explained. The word 'liturgy' is a case in point. The moment I used it I knew you'd write back and ask me to explain it. Well, here goes!

Do you remember telling me that Pat had spent most of his holiday trying to work out how you could afford to retire earlier? Well, what if I told you about a place where there was no income tax, no capital gains tax, no value added tax – in fact, no tax at all, at least as we know it? It would be good news for both of you, but unfortunately the bad news is that it no longer exists! I'm talking about ancient Athens, whose citizens were free of the 'financial furies' that pursue us throughout our lives. I know it all sounds too good to be true, because even Utopians need roads and bridges, civic buildings and public amenities. They need to protect themselves too and armies and navies don't pay for themselves. So how did they do it? They invented a unique method of public service by which every citizen was expected to be responsible for financing one major public work once in their lifetime. It might be erecting a statue, building a temple or equipping a battleship to defend their shores. When they'd done that they'd be free of any other financial responsibility for life. This act of public service performed by one person for the benefit of the whole community was called their 'liturgy'.

When Greek converts were told what Christ had done, they naturally said that this was the greatest 'liturgy' that anyone had ever performed. It was the greatest act of public service performed by one person for the good of all humanity. They didn't just want to be bystanders merely admiring what he had done, they wanted to become participators by choosing to share in his unique act of self-sacrifice themselves. Therefore, they learnt how to welcome into their lives the love already given at baptism to enable them to return that love in kind. Next they were taught how to use it to transform their own feeble love of others, until it began to resemble Christ's. Then they would have something to offer at the 'Supper of the Lord', when the greatest 'liturgy' ever would be made present in a unique way through the sacred bread and wine. This would enable them to participate in it, in such a way that they would receive to the measure of their giving. Then, to that measure they would be able to give to others as Christ had done.

This teaching was constantly repeated in the most practical way possible. Each time the believers came to participate in 'Christ's liturgy', readings from the scriptures were chosen according to the time of year, to show how Jesus had prepared to celebrate his great 'liturgy' on Calvary and the effect it had for himself and for others. This recurring cycle, in which the believer was constantly nourished by Christ's every word and deed and by his body and blood, came to be called the liturgical year. In this way believers could see and experience for themselves how Jesus tirelessly gave of himself to God and to others, and receive the strength to do likewise. So with each passing year they could enter ever more fully into his 'liturgy' both for their own personal spiritual benefit and for that of others.

When you gave up teaching you freely chose to serve God by becoming a loving wife and mother. The love that you give and the sacrifices you have made in this way are offered up in, with and through Christ each time you go to Mass. Then you receive the help and strength you need to become an ever better wife and mother as the years go by. This is how you enter into and share in the 'liturgy of Christ' – but more of this later.

I am so pleased you liked the tape* so much. I have been making a number of them recently, as there seems to be such a demand for them. Until next time.

Love,
David

* David Torkington's tapes can be ordered from: *Inner Life Tapes, 29 Chestnut Drive, Ashurst, Southampton, Hants, S040 7DW* or telephone: (023) 80292752; e-mail: ***bobbie.torkington@virgin.net*** or by contacting his website on ***http://homepage.virgin.net/david.torkington/***

29

Sacrificial Love

Dear Susanna,
I'm afraid your friend was talking through her hat. Just because Jesus never sinned it doesn't make him into a 'goody-goody' who had no idea of the trials and tribulations that the rest of us have to endure. The small temptations that we all have to experience in our daily lives can be combated fairly easily thanks to the grace of God, but really powerful temptations that few of us experience can be quite another kettle of fish.

You see, few of us who call ourselves Christians have to undergo anything like the temptations that Christ experienced, because few of us live the Christ-like life that is asked of us. Too many of us subtly lower the standards of the gospel to a level that enables us to deceive ourselves into believing that we live it; then we compromise our way through our daily lives, hardly realising what we are doing. That's why we never experience the power of evil, as Jesus did. 'We are neither hot nor cold' (Revelation 5:15). If you stand for nothing nobody will stand against you.

If you read the lives of any of the great saints you'll see how they all have to confront the power of evil again and again, and the temptations that it hurls against them. This is why Jesus taught us to pray with the words 'lead us not into temptation', because he knew from his own experience just how powerful these temptations can become. The power of evil that was bent on destroying him tested him to the limit. Reread the account of Jesus praying in Gethsemane, where the very thought of what evil was about to do to him made him sweat blood. It made him pray too for the 'chalice' of suffering to be taken away from him, though despite the fear that he felt, he repeatedly submitted to his Father's will. Precisely because Jesus never gave in to temptations more powerful than any we will experience, he felt their power more than we will ever do. Perhaps your own recent experience will help you to understand the point I'm trying to make.

Do you remember what it was like trying to give up smoking? The more you said 'no' the stronger the desire became till the only way you could get rid of it was by lighting up another cigarette. It's exactly the same with some of the more powerful temptations. The more you resist them the stronger they can get. Only giving in seems to assuage the terrible tensions involved in the struggle against them. If you want to experience just how strong such powerful temptations can be, and the strength of evil that fuels them, just keep resisting them. The next time someone treats you like a doormat say nothing. When they think you're a push-over and the bully in them treats you with contempt, grin and bear it. Then I promise you, you'll feel the power of evil rising up from within to hit back and do to them what they have done to you. Sin can often be rather like a safety-valve that prevents us from experiencing the full power of evil that's in us all. It's the saint, not the sinner, who knows just how powerful temptations can become. They believe in the power of evil, because they've experienced it for themselves far more acutely than the rest of us. That's why it's always the saint, and not the sinner, who has sympathy, understanding and compassion for those who fall, because they know only too well just how powerful temptations can be.

If you just give in to temptations you'll never experience

the power of evil as the saint does, though it will slowly possess you without you realising it. You may be extremely witty and clever, and even charming and adored by all who don't have to live with you, but you'll end up as a moral monster. Your life will be ruled by self-gratification, greed and lust, and your temper will be ruled by sudden outbursts of anger when you don't get what you want, and rampant jealousy when you see others with what you want for yourself.

Even before he called others to turn away from evil, Jesus was himself confronted by the power of evil in the desert and tempted time and time again. His repeated resistance to temptations meant that these temptations became even more potent and powerful, so that he experienced the power of evil like no other human being before or since. These temptations pursued him in different ways throughout his life on earth, and he repeatedly encountered the power of evil working particularly through those who hated and wanted to destroy him. They hated him for presenting the truth that they had twisted to their own advantage, for embodying the goodness that they had rejected, and for overflowing with the loving-kindness that had long since flowed out of them. The extent of this hatred could be seen literally and brutally embodied in Christ's bleeding and battered body that writhed with agony on the cross. Even then he was tempted to come down from that cross to confound and destroy those who had crucified him. The fact that he could have done that at any moment he chose compounded the temptations that he resisted until the end.

All these struggles and the tensions that Jesus experienced in continually facing up to the power of evil were part and parcel of the lifelong sacrifice that was offered definitively on the cross. They are part and parcel of our offering too, when we try to unite our struggles with his, our sacrifices with his, and our poor attempts at loving with his perfect loving, each time we approach the 'Sacred Mysteries'. Even our failures can be offered because in offering them we admit our weakness and show the humble and contrite heart that is necessary for all offerings to be accepted.

This is how we share in Christ's 'Liturgy of Love' – the greatest act of public service ever performed – and receive the same other-worldly love that he himself received. Then the measure in which we give and receive will be the measure in which he can continue to extend his work for the world that he has now chosen to serve through us.

Love,
David

30

Liturgy and Life

Dear Susanna,
Now you are asking too much! It would take me ages to show how the Mass as we know it developed out of the Last Supper. Books have been written about the subject and I don't intend to add to them, but at least I can try to say something that might be helpful.

Let me begin by saying that Jesus himself recognised that in freely choosing to enter into our weak human nature he needed the help and strength that only his Father could give him, just as we do, to maintain his own spiritual momentum. For this reason he structured his life in such a way that he would continually have access to that help and strength right to the end. That's why he regularly went to the temple and to the synagogue, and celebrated with his disciples the sacred meals that were an essential part of Jewish life in his day, as they are today. And that's why he often went alone for prolonged periods of personal prayer, into the inner room, into lonely places, up on the mountainside and into the garden 'where it was his custom to pray'.

Immediately after the resurrection the disciples continued to go to the synagogue and to the temple to pray, as they had done with Jesus, until the Jews threw them out as 'heretics'. But this didn't stop them going into the 'inner room' to pray as Jesus had taught them, nor did it stop them having their own prayer meetings based on the synagogue service that they'd all been brought up on. And it didn't prevent them continually celebrating the most important of all sacred meals that they had shared with Jesus on the night before he died.

The traditional synagogue service consisted of two or three readings, several prayers and a sermon or an explanation of the readings. The readings would be from the Hebrew Bible. But when the first Christians began to organise their own synagogue services for themselves they introduced new readings that were especially composed for the occasion based on the life of Jesus. These readings showed how the Old Testament writings had been perfectly fulfilled in him. Some believe that this is the origin of the gospels before they developed into the narrative form that we know today. When, later, the Creed was formulated and added, along with that ancient hymn now known as the Gloria, this service began to look distinctly like the first part of the Eucharist as we know it today. It was the custom for the Jews at that time to hold their mid-week synagogue services on Tuesdays and Thursdays, so the first Christians began to hold theirs on Wednesdays and Fridays to distinguish themselves from their compatriots who had rejected Jesus. Then, on the first day of the week, later called the 'day of the sun' or 'Sun-day', because the rising sun became a symbol of the resurrection, they celebrated what came to be called 'The Breaking of the Bread'. This was in memory of the sacred meals that they had celebrated with Jesus in the past and particularly the last and most sacred meal of all on that night before he died – the 'Last Supper'. However, because of the ever-increasing numbers of converts and the unfortunate behaviour of a few, the celebration of 'The Breaking of the Bread' in the context of an ordinary meal, as had been the custom from the beginning, was discontinued.

At first these two religious services were quite separate.

The synagogue-style service was held once or twice on weekdays, whilst 'The Breaking of the Bread' took place on Sundays. It was probably their persecution and the resulting dangers of meeting too often that led the first Christians to combine these two religious services into one. Gradually they began to meet just once a week, on Sundays, when they'd celebrate these two services together. First would be the synagogue-style service, called the synaxis, immediately followed by 'The Supper of the Lord'. From the beginning, up to the present day, this combined celebration was called the Liturgy in the Eastern Church. In the West it eventually came to be known as the Mass.

The first part of the service helped the disciples to remind themselves of all that Jesus had said and done whilst on earth, and then they prepared to receive him amongst them again, but this time as he is in heaven. That's why it was sometimes called 'The Heavenly Liturgy'. In this Jesus would be doing only one thing – endlessly loving his Father, and as he overflowed with what he received it would pass into all who would receive him. This is why he made himself present as ordinary food and drink, so that all who received him would be drawn into his new life and into the endless ecstasy of 'loving' that united him to God for eternity.

Although the first Christians devised a new Christian-style synagogue service for themselves, they couldn't build a new temple. But they didn't need one. Jesus had already made it clear that he himself was not only the new temple but also the new high priest, who had now superseded the old. In the old temple where the disciples had worshipped with Jesus during his life on earth, it would have been one of the priests, or the high priest himself, who would offer for them whatever sacrifice they wished to make. After the resurrection, however, when the old priesthood had come to an end, there was only one priesthood and one high priest, and that was Jesus himself. He didn't offer oxen or lambs or wheat or corn for others; instead he offered himself and he made it plain that this was the only offering that God wanted in future. That's why the first Christians became aware that they were all priests because only they could offer themselves, no one else could do it for them. Nevertheless, they were also aware that this offering was worthless unless it was offered in, with and through Jesus. This was the offering they made on Sundays when they came together to celebrate their sacred liturgy.

St Justin, one of the early fathers of the Church, described how the early Christians would raise the roof with the 'Great Amen' at the end of the Eucharistic Prayer when the presiding celebrant would say, 'In him, with him, and through him'. They knew only too well that the offering of their lives, their loving and their struggles had meaning only because of Jesus the 'high priest', in whom and through whom all things were offered to God.

As the Liturgy or the Mass, as we now call it, wasn't commonplace in those early days a practice gradually arose of making what, in later times, came to be called a morning offering. In this prayer everything to be done in the day ahead was offered to God so that all human endeavour could not only be sanctified but united with the sacrificial offering of Jesus. In this way the early Christians came to see that the whole of one's life, and every moment in it, could become the Mass or an endless daily liturgy – in other words, the place where we exercise our priesthood by uniting it to Christ's. This means that our homes and our places of work and recreation can become holy places because they can all become places of sacrifice.

If this means that your home becomes a place of sacrifice for you, then the bank must be the same for your husband, Pat, and the hospital for my wife, Bobbie, and my office for me. If your place of sacrifice is your home, the sacrifice you offer is primarily yourself in which your loving service as a mother and a wife is embodied. The measure in which you give will be the measure in which you receive. That's why the word 'sacrifice' literally means 'to make holy'. This is how every moment of our daily life can enable us to share in the ongoing 'Liturgy of Christ' in order to be transformed ourselves and become the means of transforming others. When we are all united in doing this together, in Christ, then the Christian Renaissance that is already overdue will at last have begun – and not before time!

Love,
David

31

Seeds of Contemplation

Dear Susanna,
Please don't feel so helpless, because you're not, far from it. Your part in this Renaissance is vital and I'm not trying to patronise or butter you up. Quite apart from your work preparing the children in your parish for Holy Communion, your role as a wife and a mother is absolutely vital. Let me explain in a little more detail exactly what I mean.

It is a historical fact that the great movements for spiritual renewal in the past did not come from the top down, but from the bottom up – from the laity, from people who first experienced the love of God that inspired them in loving homes. The great father founder of 'eremitical monasticism', St Antony, was a peasant farmer. The father founder of 'coenobitical monasticism', Pachomius, was a private soldier, and the great Macarius was a camel driver. St Francis, the father founder of the 'mendicant orders' was an assistant in the draper's shop run by his father. They were all essentially simple men, but they were learned and noble men too, like St Basil, the father founder of Eastern monasticism, for example, St Benedict, the father founder of Western monasticism, and St Bernard, who spread the great Cistercian reform all over Europe. However, whether they were simple and unlettered, or learned or of noble blood, they all had one thing in common – they came from loving homes.

The great Franciscan mystical writer St Bonaventure said that contemplation is first learnt at the mother's breast. You know what this means far better than I do for your sacrifice made sure that all your own boys were breast-fed and you know what joy this gives to a mother and the sense of security it gives to the children. When you see the open, staring eyes of a young child who has just been fed, as he or she gazes contentedly at nothing in particular, you've seen a child in contemplation. For a time at least they are filled, not only with human food, but also with the love that surrounds them. When this happens then nothing is more satisfying than simply to rest awhile and enjoy it. The Incarnation means that through your human loving your children first experience the divine.

However, I don't mean that feeding at the mother's breast is the one and only condition for future spiritual growth. That does not follow. St Bernadette, for instance, was deprived of this closeness with her mother because of a tragic accident. Her mother's breasts were badly burnt from a falling candle that set fire to her clothes, but this did not prevent Bernadette eventually attaining sanctity. The point I want to emphasise is that the seeds of contemplation are sown in a loving home with a loving mother and father. Later the child will want to explore the world around them and become lost in endless activity. Nevertheless, once these seeds have been sown that child will always be able to see beyond the world that tempted them to leave the security of their home. It will enable them to find through that world the One who first created it and who still speaks through his creation to those who are open enough to hear him.

This is why any vocation director worth his salt will always visit the homes of those who wish to become priests or religious to see if the foundations have been laid that will enable a prospective vocation to flourish. Before the contemplation that can alone support the priest or religious of the future, purification must precede it, and that can be daunting for anyone. It is easier for those who have already known the security of a loving family, where they first experienced the love of God through their parents, to survive this difficult and testing time, though even they will need help and advice. The great religious leaders and saints of the future, who are needed to bring about a 'Christian Renaissance', will find their task less daunting if they have first experienced the love of God in loving homes, and most of all from a loving mother. They may later reject some of the standards of their parents, as St Francis did, but they will never reject the love that they first received through them.

From all this, I hope you can see how absolutely vital your role is in helping to bring about this Renaissance. As your children grow up you must not only continue to give them the love they need, but the example that will speak to them more than any words of what you believe and what you wish to share with them. This is why you need to pray, to turn to God daily for the super-human help that only he can give to enable you to be an ever-loving wife and mother.

Love,
David

32

A Community of Love

Dear Susanna,
I am pleased that you found what I said helpful. It is sad that so little has been taught about the mystery of motherhood and marriage in our schools and from our pulpits. Once again it is misguided beliefs that are responsible for distorting the authentic Judaeo-Christian attitude towards sexuality and marriage from the earliest centuries up to the present day. I am sure that when you look back on your school days you will remember how you received little if any advice to prepare you for motherhood and marriage, and how questions affecting sexuality were avoided like the plague by teachers who simply did not know how to handle them.

Do you remember the case of a girl in your school who was given two weeks' detention for 'unspecified crimes'? I became involved because of my friendship with her parents. It seems that the comedian of the class had got her to ask the sister who was teaching them religion to describe exactly what was involved in circumcision. The sister turned bright red and rushed out of the classroom straight to the Reverend Mother. It's sad that such a ruse, which must have been played out in many a convent school over the years, caused such embarrassment.

This highlights just how far heretical viewpoints have perverted the sense of the sacred that surrounded sexuality in the scriptures. When God promised Abraham that he would become the father of a great nation he insisted that that promise should be enshrined in the bodies of all his male descendants, so that the very act by which the seed would be handed on should be sanctified. What could be more sacred than for a man to become a collaborator with God in bringing about his promises – and for a woman too, who received the sacred seed in her womb? It's not surprising, then, that virginity had no positive meaning in the Old Testament, because it would inevitably mean exclusion from this sacred co-operation with God.

In this context, Mary's virginity would not have been seen as a blessing but as a curse, had God himself not called her to virginity so that he could make her fruitful with the seed of his own love. In future, virginity would not automatically be seen as a curse by God, because it may well involve a special call to spiritual pregnancy by the power of the same Holy Spirit who brought Christ to birth in Mary. In the new covenant the call to marriage and the call to virginity would stand side by side as two distinct but equal vocations. They would both, but in different ways, enable people to co-operate with God in transmitting the seeds of the Kingdom, once promised to a particular race, to the whole human race. The balance that made these equal but different vocations, however, was soon destroyed by influences totally at variance with an authentic biblical spirituality. These influences took the form of two insidious heresies – Neo-Platonism from the West and Manicheism from the East. Both denounced the body as evil and as the source of all human corruption. From this it's easy to see how virginity soon came to be seen as the perfect state and marriage a less perfect and even positively dangerous state. The way of perfection and the way of virginity soon came to be seen as synonymous, and therefore the way that one would expect all priests to follow if they would avoid the evils 'that the flesh is heir to'. This is why so many people, particularly priests of the 'old school', still find it difficult to accept the idea of married priests. The first Christians had no such difficulty until pagan ideas began to distort and disfigure what God had made holy.

Christianity has never fully been able to free itself from this pernicious vein of mistaken Puritanism that has distorted it from its beginning to the present day. It has been particularly apparent in some highly suspect and even unsavoury forms of asceticism, that often seem to border on masochism, and in the prudish and prurient view of marriage and human sexuality that is totally at variance with the scriptures. Far from rectifying this attitude to the body, reformers have not only accepted it without question, but even condemned the body further by declaring it intrinsically evil, like its owner, and therefore unredeemable. The divine life, they argued, couldn't possibly enter into a corrupt human nature to redeem it from within; it could only shine brightly through the merits of Christ and thus be 'covered up', in such a way that God won't take account of it.

The rise of the socio-psychological sciences, together with the new biblical theology, that had their origins in the last century and were more fully developed in this century, were deeply influential. They enabled the Church to restate the true biblical meaning of marriage and the sacred and sacramental character of sexuality that has been for too long perverted. When teachers can explain this to their pupils without embarrassment then it will be a sign that an important step towards a Christian Renaissance will have taken place. For no such Renaissance will have any deep or lasting effect without a renewal of what the Vatican Council called the 'domestic Church'. It is here, in the home, that the liturgy of selflessness and sacrifice is first learnt, and it is the place where married couples minister to each other the seeds of God's love that will enable them to seek and find the fullness of love to which they have both been called.

Love,
David

33

The Domestic Church

Dear Susanna,
I heard a very interesting interview on the radio last night. It was the last in a series called 'Devout Sceptics'. Bel Mooney was interviewing the actor Simon Russell Beale. It seems that he was brought up as a practising Christian and went to church at least once a day until his early twenties when he began to lapse into the scepticism from which he's never fully emerged. When asked whether or not he believed in grace he immediately answered, 'Yes, because I love and am loved'. However, when Bel Mooney went on to ask whether or not he believed in God's grace he retreated into his scepticism.

His failure to see that the two cannot be easily separated highlights one of the most serious failures in Christian teaching from the earliest times, thanks to the heresies I mentioned in my last letter. Hadn't St John made it quite clear that wherever there is love then there is God? After all, this is the whole meaning of the 'good news'. It is simply that the fullness of love that has no beginning and no ending has entered into space and time, into human flesh and blood, so that we can experience in part something of the fullness that we are all called to hereafter.

If we are going to experience some sort of redemption from the moral morass that muddies the lives of the best of us, then pure, unalloyed love is our only hope. Giving and receiving love is the most sacred vocation to which all are called, and marriage is the place where the vast majority of us live out that vocation. How tragic, then, that this sacred place has been spoiled by heresies that seeped into some of the best minds in Christendom from the very beginning. Many of the greatest Christian writers were deceived into believing that the body is in some way evil and the prison of the soul, preventing it from rising to God. Even a great mystical writer like St Gregory of Nyssa, for instance, referred to marriage as 'a sad tragedy', one of the regrettable results of original sin. St Ambrose called it 'a galling burden'. St Jerome believed that its only positive significance was that it raised virgins with which to adorn the Church! Although Saint Augustine's view is well known – that sexual intimacy is always sinful except for procreation – it is not so well known that St Gregory the Great went one step further, condemning all sexual intercourse for whatever reason as inevitably sinful. What was holy and sacred for Jesus and the Jewish tradition into which he was born suddenly became suspect, ugly or even evil because of misguided attitudes that have desecrated the concept of Christian marriage for centuries.

It's no wonder that it took almost a thousand years before theologians began to debate seriously whether or not marriage was a sacrament and five hundred more before it was declared one at the Council of Trent just over four hundred years ago. Even then the Council was primarily concerned with condemning the reformers, and little in the way of a positive theology of marriage developed until the Second Vatican Council. Then, at last, the family was described as 'a community of love' in which the mutual love of the couple not only ministers Christ's love to each other, but through this into the wider world. History had turned full circle when, far from being seen as an inevitable occasion of sin, the Council proclaimed the marital act a unique means of grace.

Sadly, endless debates about contraception and other questions of sexual ethics have prevented a positive theology of marriage emerging after Vatican II. Such a theology is needed to filter down and sustain what the Council called 'the domestic Church' with a rich and positive spirituality from which it has been starved for centuries. It is insufficient to educate the young about the 'facts of life' and the Church's teaching on sexual morality without at the same time opening them to a positive and practical spirituality for married life. They ought to be shown that the formal liturgy of the wedding is but the public proclamation of two complementary human beings, who commit themselves to 'minister' to each other the divine love through their human loving, for the rest of their lives. In this way the two are drawn ever more deeply into one another as they are drawn into God. Young people need to be taught about the various stages of each couple's life together, with an appreciation of each other's emotional and sexual needs, in the context of sacramental grace. Then they will be the better prepared for the sacred ministry upon which the future Church depends more than any other. For no Renaissance will have any deep or lasting effect without a Renaissance of the 'domestic Church' where the liturgy of selflessness and sacrifice is first learnt.

Love,
David

34

The Sacrament of Touch

Dear Susanna,
I saw a documentary on the television a week or two ago about a fascinating archaeological find. It seems that the Holy Land experienced one of its hottest summers on record in 1986. The water level in the Sea of Galilee sank, revealing large areas of mud that had never been seen in living memory. Something else was revealed in that mud that had never been seen before. It was an ancient fishing boat, 20 feet long by 7 feet wide. It was dragged out of the mud and taken to a nearby kibbutz where it was cleaned down and then carbon-dated. It was found to be about two thousand years old and designed to carry between 12 and 15 fishermen – so the locals called it the 'Jesus boat'. Although very little seems to have been done to restore it in the intervening years, it has been thoroughly cleaned and treated with wax which has seeped into its timbers and preserved it, enabling it to be put on permanent display.

When a group of tourists were being shown the boat recently, a young man asked if he could touch it. The archaeologist on duty explained that it was not permitted. However, when he admitted that he had touched the boat himself in the course of his work, the young man immediately touched him, and his fellow pilgrims followed suit. It all happened so naturally, so spontaneously, that it demonstrated a deep belief that something precious can be communicated by touch.

This is a conviction that is at the heart of the gospel story, which begins with a very special touch – the touch of God. When the 'finger of God's right hand' touched the Virgin Mary she conceived by the power of the Holy Spirit so that the love of God himself was made flesh within her womb. As the Son of God grew 'in wisdom and understanding' under the influence of the love that had conceived him in the first place, he was able to communicate to others something of what he had received by his own sacred touch. It enabled him to heal and make whole and even raise from the dead. Although he was moved by compassion to help people in their physical need, the power of his love that could be seen by all symbolised a far deeper spiritual power, one that could bring not just physical but spiritual healing too and inner transformation. This spiritual power was handed on to the first apostles so that they too could pass on to others what they had received from the Lord himself.

It was a sacred and holy touch used by the apostles and their successors to hand down to successive generations the love that had been received by Jesus in the fullest possible way on the first Easter Day. This is why touch is so important in the rites of Christian initiation. It means that the love of Christ that was communicated to you at baptism had been literally handed on for almost two thousand years. Through this sacred touch you were given the very love of God that could be transformed into ever more perfect human loving to reach out from you to others. When you met Pat this loving was able to be refined and purified further, most especially when you committed yourselves to each other for life in the 'sacrament of touch'. The loving touch of the married couple becomes the means by which the divine is communicated through the human to each other and then on to their children. The power of this love is, however, dependent on the selflessness with which it is both given and received as their lives unfold.

When my own parents turned to their spiritual director for help in their marriage, they were fortunate to have a holy man as well as a man of great learning to guide them. He explained to them how the most sacred moment in the 'sacrament of touch' is when the couple are bonded to one another in every possible way here on earth. Then they give to each other their hearts, their minds and their bodies as a means of giving their inner selves through a union that will grow ever deeper and bond them ever more fully into each other in their mutual journey into perfect love.

He taught them how to savour these moments, as one should savour the bodily union with Jesus in the sacred ministry. He explained to them that, when they had reached the climax of their loving, they should remain still, side by side, to assimilate and digest what they had both given and both received. He even tempered my mother's enthusiasm for early rising to go to the sacrament in the church when the sacrament of their marriage could be celebrated in their own home with the minister she had been leaving behind. You can minister Christ to each other where you are, he told them, by exercising the sacrament to which you have both committed yourselves.

What was received in these sacred moments led them both into a deep interior peace, not only immediately after the sacred celebrations, but throughout the rest of the day as the profound peace that they experienced began to permeate the rest of their lives. There is no other sacrament that so embodies the mystery of the Incarnation as the sacrament of marriage, to which most of us are called and in which the majority of us are first formed.

Love,
David

35

Martha and Mary

Dear Susanna,
I'm so sorry the sermon upset you. Most sermons on the story of Martha and Mary seem to give the wrong impression. They make many mothers like yourself feel like second-class citizens in the Church, because they don't seem to have the time for prayer that they feel is expected of them.

The first thing I would like to say to you is that this particular story has been repeatedly misinterpreted. A simple and self-evident observation made by Jesus was taken out of context by some, to endorse the religious life at the expense of the married life. When you see this story in the context of the whole of the gospels such an interpretation cannot be sustained.

Now the old penny catechism defined prayer as 'the raising of the heart and the mind to God'. There are two ways of doing this – first by turning to God directly in formal prayer, and then secondly by turning to him indirectly through the neighbour in need. Your immediate neighbour is your family who are in need of your love, your care and your attention. When you turn to them in selfless loving service you are turning to God who identifies himself with the neighbour in need. After all, charity begins at home, even though it doesn't end there.

The Bible tells us that at the last judgement God doesn't ask those he is about to judge how much time they spent in formal prayer, what wonderful feelings they had there, or how many ecstasies they experienced. He says quite clearly and quite emphatically, 'How did you love me in the neighbour in need?' In your case, the first neighbours in need of your attention are your own children. When you spend your time trying to feed and clothe them, trying to free them from the insecurities and the fears that imprison them, then you are doing it for God.

Different ways of life make different demands on the amount of time that needs to be given to formal prayer. A religious living alone, for instance, can easily become insular and self-centred. Greater time therefore would be necessary for formal prayer. This enables him or her to practise the selfless giving that is more readily open to a mother. It also enables the religious to receive directly the same love that a mother receives indirectly from her children and her husband. On the other hand, every mother also needs time for formal prayer to practise selfless giving, as I will explain later, and to receive the help and strength she needs too for her special and demanding vocation. This will enable her to continue giving herself to her children with the selfless sacrificial love that will make her a good mother and will enable them to be confident and loving children.

A great medieval mystic called Angela of Foligno, who was a mother before she became a religious, readily admitted that she needed more time for formal prayer when she was a religious than when she was a mother. She found that she was far more in danger of falling into selfishness in the convent than she had been looking after her children in her own home. She also learnt from her spiritual father, St Francis, and from her own personal experience, that the more she gave as a mother, or as a religious for that matter, then the more she received the love that she desired more than anything else. As St Francis put it, 'It is in giving that you receive'.

Sometimes religious people give the impression that God calls especially chosen 'souls' to the religious life while the rest of us, who are encumbered with bodies, have to muddle through in the married or the single life, as if vocation meant only one thing. If God calls each of us to different vocations in life, he certainly does not categorise them in order of priority, as if some were spiritually more perfect or more important than others. That sort of spiritual categorising owes far more to Neo-Platonism and Manicheism than to the gospels. All vocations are important, but in different ways. It's not a matter of being a Martha or a Mary; it's a matter of being both. The balance between the two must always be determined by each person's respective vocation in life and this may change with the years.

Jesus himself was 'busy about many things' (Luke 2:49), doing his father's will, but he still needed time for the prayer that led him to 'the inner room', to 'lonely places', and to 'the garden where it was his custom to pray'. In him we find the perfect balance as a model for those of us who are called to the active life. Need we look any further?

Love,
David

36

Practical Priesthood

Dear Susanna,
All that is involved in your particular vocation as a wife, as a mother and as a sometime teacher should be the subject of what I called your morning offering. This is how you unite yourself with the offering of Jesus in and through all you do each day.

I was taught the morning offering at primary school too. We were told that it would make us into 'little priests' because it would enable us to offer up every thing that we did, just like Jesus. The trouble was, the teacher explained it in the context of the story of 'Rumpelstiltskin' and so I got the wrong idea. She said that just as Rumpelstiltskin could change a room full of straw into gold, the morning offering could change a daily mess into a daily Mass. The upshot of this was that I saw it as a magic formula that once said had the desired effect without the need to do anything further. The truth of the matter is it will inevitably degenerate into a sort of magic formula if a person is led to believe that its daily repetition will automatically change the forthcoming day. If it is going to have the desired effect, the offering should be followed by a spiritual training session to practise the selfless giving that can alone transform what could otherwise be a daily mess into a daily Mass. This training session has traditionally been called 'morning prayer'.

Now I don't want to say anything about the content of

morning prayer, which needn't last for more than five or ten minutes, because you've already read the suggestions I've made in my books *The Hermit* and *Inner Life.* The point I want to make here is that no matter what means of prayer you choose, you'll inevitably find that even in only five minutes you could well have fifty-five distractions, or more, and as many temptations, too, to pack it all in to do something more practical. Nevertheless, please believe me that there's nothing more practical that you could possibly do than this.

You see, if you freely choose to turn away from what you would like to think or fantasise about in order to turn your attention back to God, you are in fact practising selflessness. There is no more important lesson that could be learnt. As a trained teacher yourself, you know as well as I do that the habits that are necessary to acquire any skill are formed by performing a series of actions, and learning selflessness is no exception to the rule. In other words, as a result of performing a series of selfless actions you gradually develop a habit of selflessness that will make you into a better mother and wife, and a better neighbour too.

Prayer, whatever form it may take, always provides a place for practising selflessness, as you endlessly find yourself trying to turn your attention away from distractions and back to God – or, to use the biblical word again, repenting. I even think you could convince a confirmed atheist of the importance of prayer by showing how it can be used to teach a person to become more human. Surely it stands to reason that the more selfless someone becomes the more loving and more lovable they become too, and if that doesn't make them more human, what does?

However, genuine Christian prayer is much more than this, because as God is always turned towards us and open to us, the very moment we turn and try to remain open to him, his love automatically begins to pour into us. In other words, he gives as we give and what he gives is the help and strength needed to become more and more perfect, more and more Christ-like. In this way, prayer time becomes the time when we learn to be ever more selfless, and therefore, in your case, an ever more caring and compassionate wife and mother.

I can almost hear you say, 'Well, that's all very well and good, but where on earth am I going to find the time? After all, can't I learn to be selfless as I look after my children every hour of the day, every day of the week?' There's a lot of truth in that, but isn't it also true that although you exercise your body doing the daily chores, you still see the need for having set periods of time each day on your exercise machine? You feel physically better after the training session and you feel the benefit of it throughout the rest of your day too.

It's exactly the same with prayer, where you exercise the muscles of your heart and mind. It will help you develop a habit of selflessness that will enable you to act selflessly throughout the rest of the day with ever greater ease and facility. In short, it will do for your 'soul' what physical exercise can do for your body. This is the best possible way of transforming the morning offering from a genuine desire into practice throughout the rest of the day. This is how, in the words of my primary school teacher, what would otherwise be a daily mess can be transformed into a daily Mass. That's what the priesthood we share in Christ means and that's the most important way we exercise it.

Love,
David

37

Oiling the Muscles

Dear Susanna,
Of course I've fallen asleep at prayer. It's usually because I was tired out before I even started. If you're too tired to pray it means you need rest. Even one of the strictest and most ascetical of all mystics, St Peter of Alcantara, advised anyone too tired to pray to go back to bed and catch up on their sleep, then begin again. However, having said that, prayer itself can be very tiring, especially when it turns out to be a continual battle against distractions.

What you've got to remember is that when you start to pray seriously and systematically from scratch you are beginning to exercise the muscles of the heart and mind that have hardly been used in this way before. So naturally you'll find it not only difficult, but very tiring too.

I went on holiday to Menorca last May and was so delighted to find that our hotel had a swimming pool that I overdid things. I forgot it was twenty years since I'd done any serious swimming and swam for length after length. I didn't sleep that night. I was over-tired and muscles that had been holidaying for twenty years began to complain all night long and well into the following week. Prayer cannot only be difficult but tiring if you have never prayed seriously for years, if ever before. So take things easy to begin with.

Yes, it is important to give a set period of time to prayer each day, but to begin with make it no more than five to ten minutes. You'll not only be able to pray more easily, but even enjoy it once your spiritual muscles have been loosened up and gently exercised by practice.

The time element is very important. Once you've decided on giving a set time each day, you must stick to your resolution, come hell or high water. It's essential to give the same time to prayer whether you feel like it or whether you don't, so that your regularity, particularly when you don't feel like it, demonstrates before you even begin that you are primarily there for God, not for what you get out of him. When cupboard-love ends, real selfless prayer begins, and this opens you up to receive what you never even imagined possible at the beginning.

Never think for a moment that endless distractions prevent you from praying, when in fact the contrary is true. St Teresa of Avila admitted that she rarely prayed without distractions. When God granted her special mystical experiences like 'full union' or 'ecstasy' she didn't have any distractions at all, because these experiences were pure gifts of God in whom she was totally absorbed. However, not even she could really call these experiences prayer in the strict sense of the word, because she was doing nothing and God was doing everything.

So true prayer takes place in between the time when you fall asleep, and are therefore doing nothing, and ecstasy, when God is doing everything. This time is always full of far more distractions than you would choose. Once again you can see that prayer is the place where we practise acting selflessly, where we practise turning back to God through the repentance that opens us up to receive his love in the very act of turning and opening to receive it.

Some years ago our boat got trapped in an old lock that opened on to a vast reservoir. Although we managed to close the gate behind us we couldn't open the lock gate that would admit us to the reservoir. Try as best I could to turn the handle that would open the gate, I simply got nowhere. The whole mechanism had seized up with dust and rust and we simply didn't know what to do, until Bobbie suddenly had an idea. As I tried once more, she poured oil on to the cogs and slowly but surely, with my efforts and the facilitating power of the oil, I was able to turn the handle and the gates began to open. Then gradually the water from the reservoir poured in to rescue us. Exactly the same thing happens in prayer. As we try to turn our attention back to God, despite the muscles that have seized up with under-use, the Holy Spirit infiltrates our poor human endeavour, gradually easing and facilitating what would have been quite impossible without him.

That's why oil is used in the sacraments as a sign of the way the love of God is always available and ready to penetrate the innermost recesses of our minds and hearts so that they can turn to him with ever-increasing ease. This profound spiritual process continues until we have one heart and mind with him. Then we can begin to experience something of the ecstasy of life at its fullest, an ecstasy that has been God's experience from the beginning and which he wants us to share with him for eternity.

Love,
David

38

Props for Prayer

Dear Susanna,
I couldn't agree with you more. Some people do treat their favourite methods of prayer like magic formulas that will invariably have the desired effect, which is usually to get what they want out of God. Different ways, methods or techniques of prayer are only means to an end. St John of the Cross used the story of Moses to make this point.

After he had sent Joshua to engage the Amalekites in battle, Moses took up his position on the hillside to pray for victory. As long as his arms remain outstretched Joshua had the upper hand, but as soon as weariness forced him to lower them then the Amalekites began to prosper. Noticing this, his brothers propped up his arms until sunset, assuring victory to their army!

These physical props symbolised for St John the spiritual props, or methods of prayer, that we all need to help keep our hearts and minds raised and open to God. They are therefore means to this end and should be used as such. This means there is no one perfect method, just different ways for each person at different stages of their spiritual journey. What helps a person at the outset of their journey may not help them as they get into their stride. What helped them when they were going downhill with the wind at their back might be of little use when they are struggling uphill with the wind in their face. What helped them in the spring might not help them in the autumn of their life.

A spiritual director can be of great help, but one who insists on forcing their own preferred method of prayer on you and on everyone else 'willy-nilly' is most certainly bogus. What would you think if your local GP insisted on handing out pink pills to all who walked into the surgery without at least trying to find out their needs? You'd undoubtedly think that the GP was a quack – and you'd be right.

A genuine spiritual director will try to assess where you are on the journey and try to suggest, but never impose, the means of prayer best suited to your needs, knowing that what may be of help today may be of little help tomorrow. If you want me to make suggestions to help you then I'll be looking to you to give me the lead and depend on you to tell me honestly whether or not the advice I give is of any help. But before I make any suggestions please try to give me some idea of where you stand at the present so that I may be able to be of more practical assistance.

Before I sign off there's something else I want to draw to your attention from the story of Moses at prayer. The longer he was able to remain open to the action of God the more God was able to enter not only into him, but through him into the people for whom he prayed. In other words, when we pray successfully for someone in need God answers that prayer not by bypassing us and acting independently but by acting through us. This means that the more open to God a person is the more effective their prayer, as God acts through them with greater ease and efficiency than through a person saturated with selfishness.

We had to have a new boiler, several pipes and three radiators replaced because they had furred up, preventing the water circulating with the efficiency that it had before. It's a bit like that with the spiritual life. That's why we turn to people who we recognise as better than ourselves to pray for us. That's why whenever there's news of a person of genuine sanctity anywhere in the world, people flock to them for their help and for their prayers, and that's why people turn to saints to pray and intercede for them. Intuitively we know that when we are all furred up with selfishness and sin the love of God cannot flow into and through us with the speed and efficiency that we would like.

The conclusion is simple. There's nothing magical about prayer. The more we pray, practising the selflessness that purifies our spiritual arteries, the more the love of God can flow in and around every part of us. Then it can flow through us to reach those we love and those for whom we pray. Its effectiveness depends on both the love of God and the quality of the person who prays. The more they've done to purify their spiritual arteries of the selfishness that furs them up, then the more perfectly can the divine work through the human. This is how prayer enables God to work through us to reach out to those for whom we pray, and even to those we have not prayed for, whom he chooses to reach out to through us.

Love,
David

39

From God with Love

Dear Susanna,
Thank you for being so honest with me about your own inner journey and your prevailing state of spiritual darkness. I can well understand why you ended your letter wondering why on earth God wanted to create us in the first place. Strangely enough the answer to this question will help shed some light on your present darkness. Sadly, we only have our own limited experience to help us unravel this great mystery, but it's all we have, so let's try to make the best of it.

Imagine the most thrilling and exciting experience of pure selfless loving that you have ever known. Then multiply it by as many times as your imagination will allow, to give you the best possible glimpse of the love that God continually experiences. His very existence is a continual conscious ecstasy that gives him unalloyed and endless delight.

Next, imagine yourself alone, revelling in something that moves you deeply. It might be a brilliant theatrical performance, an unforgettable sunset or some other experience that thrills you through and through. No matter how great your joy, it will be marred, because it is not shared, particularly by those you love most. This may help you to appreciate, if not understand, why God wanted to extend his own experience of pure spiritual joy to others.

As nothing can exist outside of him, his 'Other self' whom our tradition calls the 'Word', would be transformed into another dimension as the 'Masterwork' of a parallel physical creation. All things would exist in him and for him and would share, to the measure of their capacity, in the love that animates God to eternity. This is what St John explains in the prologue to the gospel that proclaims Christ not just as God's physical masterwork, but as the King of all creation over which he came to reign and with whom he came to share his glory. This is a vision that is revealed to and experienced by the 'poor and lowly' who make their lives over to God. A man like St Francis of Assisi, for instance, was able to see further and deeper than the greatest philosophers whose ultimate vision was obscured by too much complexity. He saw, in simple terms, that all things were created in the man he called 'Friar Jesus'. The world, therefore, must be a friary and everything in it brother and sister to one another. Not just Brother Francis and Sister Clare, but Brother fire and Sister water, Brother wolf and Sister rabbit, Brother sun and Sister moon. This enabled his devoted follower, the great British theologian John Duns Scotus, to express in the language of his trade the vision of Francis that turned received wisdom on its head and returned to the wisdom of St John.

Christ the 'Masterwork', 'in whom all things had been created from the beginning' (read John 1 and Colossians 1) didn't or couldn't have come as an afterthought. He was God's first thought. God wasn't forced to send him because of man's sin, his so-called 'felix culpa', but because of his infinite love that he wanted to share. It had always been God's plan to create a world in space and time, of matter and form and of men and women, not just in Christ but for him so that he could enter into that world as its crowning glory. Nevertheless, when Christ came it was not to celebrate, but to commiserate with a people who had fallen from grace as God had never intended.

The intended celebration would have to be postponed indefinitely, until humankind could be rescued from what had been its undoing. Now Christ had a new role, never originally intended. He had to explain to everyone what had happened to them. Then he had to inspire them to turn back to the only love that would restore them to the full human stature that all could see embodied and then brought to perfection in him. Only this would enable them to experience the fullness of life for which they had been created.

The reason for your darkness is because you have already listened to Christ, turned to him and allowed the light of his love to reach out to you. When this light first strikes, the mystics call it 'a ray of darkness' because it highlights all that prevents you from being united with God and experiencing the joy for which he created you. You see, unlike things cannot be united, so the Spirit who unites God to his 'Word' must prepare you for union with them both through a profound purification. Only through this second 'baptism of fire' can he prepare you to be taken up into the mystery of love to experience the ecstasy of life at its fullest for eternity. That's why, after what seemed to be early success in prayer, you've come to this inexplicable impasse.

Next time I want to begin to show you the way forward, till then –

Love,
David

40

Learning to Love

Dear Susanna,
No, I don't think I'm misunderstanding your predicament, but I think you are. If you won't listen to me perhaps you'll listen to St John of the Cross, who was made a Doctor of the Church because of his profound insights into the spiritual life and, most important, into prayer life. He makes it quite plain that virtually everyone who takes prayer seriously and who gives regular and daily time to personal prayer, whether they feel like it or whether they don't, will eventually find themselves in your predicament. In other words, they'll come to the point where they'll find that they can no longer meditate as they once did, nor do they feel inclined to do so, despite a deep yearning that makes them mourn for their maker who seems to have turned his back on them.

The most frightening thing he has to say is that ninety per cent of people who come to this point give up regular daily prayer for good. This disturbing statistic is sadly verified today, though in my personal experience the percentage is even higher. We no longer have a reformed Carmelite Order, or any other for that matter, who are dedicated to helping travellers at this particular point in the spiritual journey.

St John's works were written, not for complete beginners, but precisely for people like you, to help them journey on to be purified for union with God in what he called the 'The Dark Night of the Soul'. He gave it this title because the prayer that had once seemed to be full of sweetness and light suddenly seemed to be full of bitterness and darkness. It's easy to be with Christ when he is giving out free food, working miracles and raising people from the dead – that's not difficult. But are we prepared to suffer with him? Are we prepared to go into the desert with him, into the inner room, into Gethsemane to be tempted with him and to struggle against the power of evil which we find lurking deep down within? It is this that prevents us from attaining the union to which we aspire more than anything else.

Your experience of prayer in the charismatic movement is typical. What is not necessarily typical, however, was your daily faithfulness to personal prayer as well as to the community prayer that you shared at the charismatic meetings. Believe me, not all charismatics do this. Those who do will always come to the same predicament in which you now find yourself. Those who don't will go on for a lifetime seeking nice feelings and spiritual goodies, but they will never journey on into the 'Dark Night' where they will alone be purified for what, or rather for whom, they have been created.

The whole point of the new predicament in which you now find yourself is that you are now being offered the opportunity of becoming a spiritual adult. In other words, you are being given the opportunity of learning pure selfless love. This is the love that goes on giving when nothing seems to be received in return. It's the sort of loving that will make you into an even better wife and mother.

Marriages are falling apart all round us today because people have been brought up in a culture of instant gratification. Many are no longer prepared to work at their relationships, to go on giving and loving and making sacrifices for the other. In short, they no longer know what loving is all about. Several generations have been brainwashed by the media into accepting a squalid little equation that seems to be implicit in the newspapers they read, the television they watch or the films they revel in. The equation is this: love = sexual pleasure. And so many have swallowed it 'hook, line and sinker' without realising it.

Whether a person is married or not, the moment they cease to get the pleasure they originally received from their partner's body, they think that love has broken down. Then they think it is time to seek out another body to turn them on again to what they wrongly believe to be love. For the same reason, the vast majority of people give up spiritual loving in prayer the moment they no longer receive exhilarating spiritual experiences in return.

Marriages, whether spiritual or physical, succeed when people are prepared to work at them by learning how to become more and more selfless, more concerned about giving than receiving. This is what is being asked of you now in prayer. If you are prepared to go on come what may, you'll not only learn selflessness in prayer but what you've learnt there will enable you to become a more tolerant, more patient and more loving wife and mother outside of prayer. This will in turn open you both inside and outside of prayer to receive a quality of loving that you have never dreamt possible before. It will change not only you, but everyone around you – those whom you love and even those whom you don't.

Love,
David

41

Speed Training

Dear Susanna,
The biggest temptation for someone in your predicament is to believe that they're wasting their time – but believe me, you're not! I know it seems futile spending a quarter of an hour endlessly battling against distractions, but you are in effect not just learning selflessness, as I've explained, but learning to act selflessly with ever greater speed. Let me explain what I mean.

The buzzword amongst sports coaches at the moment is 'speed training'. The theory is simply common sense. You might be wonderful with the ball at your feet, or in your hands, you might have a brilliant backhand and a superlative smash, but if you don't get to the ball in time your skills will be superfluous. Speed training is of the utmost importance in the spiritual life too. I mentioned only a few weeks ago that the difference between saints and ourselves is not that we sin and they didn't, but the speed with which they sought forgiveness. Sometimes it takes days, weeks, months or even years before we have the humility to accept that we have fallen and then seek the forgiveness we need before beginning again. In this way we waste time that could have been saved if only we had the same sort of humility that enabled the saints to begin again without delay the very moment they were conscious of falling. Long before modern coaches realised the importance of 'speed training' it was practised by the saints who knew that it was the only way to sanctity. They found by their own experience that it is not easy to begin again without delay, without the 'speed training' that they knew could only be learnt in prayer.

What they came to realise is that by turning away from distractions without delay, they could practise inside of prayer the speed that they needed to turn back to God outside of prayer whenever they fell. Furthermore they received the grace to enable them to do this with ever-increasing ease at the same time.

The word 'ascetic' comes from the Greek word for an athlete, because a Christian ascetic is a spiritual athlete, who practises again and again the discipline necessary to enable them to turn back to God as often as they turn away from him. Christian athletes must give more time to training than their secular counterparts because they are developing the most important muscles that any human being possesses. While Olympic athletes spend hours practising developing the muscles in the arms and legs, in the neck and down the back, Christian athletes spend their time developing the muscles of their hearts and minds.

Prayer is the gymnasium or the training ground where the most important human muscles are exercised time and again as Christian athletes turn to raise their hearts to God, despite the distractions that might prevent them. Like any new form of exercise it is difficult at first because the muscles that are being used have not developed fully. But in time and with perseverance, what was initially and understandably difficult becomes easier, so that the habit of instantly turning back to God is learnt inside of prayer in such a way that it can be put into daily practice outside of prayer.

However, Christian athletes develop these muscles not only to raise their hearts and minds to God, but to open them to him too, so that his love can enter into them. This enables God to give power and strength to the receiver so that their spiritual muscles act with ever greater ease. It is in this profound interchange of love that takes place in prayer that a person's heart is gradually changed, so that it can turn to God more swiftly both inside and outside of prayer. In time and with perseverance, the heart is able to remain raised and open to God for longer periods of time and the longer it remains open to him the more it comes under his influence. What at first seemed no more than a gentle pull becomes like an increasingly stronger magnetic force as God begins to draw not just the heart but the whole person into a profound mystical experience of his presence. What was traditionally called 'discursive prayer' now becomes contemplative. Now the Christian athlete has reached such a point of spiritual fitness that God is in their hearts and minds continually in such a way that they can experience his presence as never before.

This does not mean that they will no longer fall, but the moment they do they are able to turn back to God with a speed and urgency that they never achieved before. They cannot bear to be separated for a moment from the One whose love they have experienced enveloping their whole being. 'Speed training' has done its work, as it always will for those who choose to practise it. So whatever you do, please don't give up prayer, for what you learn there cannot be learnt elsewhere.

Love,
David

42

Weight Training

Dear Susanna,
I'm pleased you see the point I was trying to make about 'speed training', but this time I want to talk to you about another form of training that's 'old hat' today. It's called 'weight training'. It's not that it is out of fashion now – far from it; it's simply taken for granted today. In my day it was the latest thing and it made a dramatic difference to those who made use of it.

Its advantages had already been realised in the USA in the thirties and the forties. However, it took a couple of decades before it caught on and its practice became widespread in Britain. Like speed training, the principle behind it was very simple. By repeatedly raising weights above your head you were developing not just the muscles in your arms and legs, but virtually every other muscle in your body simultaneously. This meant that the whole person was not only made stronger and more powerful, but also gained powers of endurance. Even people who were naturally gifted, or who had a high degree of technical training, soon realised that they would end up the losers if they didn't also take up weight training.

Now the amazing thing was that, given the necessary technical 'know-how', a powerful super-athlete could be fashioned by one single action repeated over and over again. Once again the analogy is a perfect demonstration of how Christian athletes or ascetics are formed in the spiritual life when they practise the raising of their hearts to God in prayer. What they came to realise was that as they performed this single action they were developing and strengthening not only the muscles of their hearts but other spiritual muscles too at one and the same time. The interesting and consoling thing for all of us is that they came to realise too that when this spiritual weight lifting became difficult then their prayer became more and more effective.

In other words, when you continually try to raise your heart to God even though, or I should say especially when, you don't feel he is loving you, then you learn the selfless sacrificial love that was perfectly embodied in Jesus Christ himself. When your mind wrongly tells you that there is no one listening yet you nevertheless continue to pray as best you can, then the muscles of your mind are developed ever more fully too, so that your faith will eventually be able to move far more than mere mountains. And when spiritual darkness makes you feel helpless and hopeless and yet you still keep trying to raise your heart to God, you learn to hope beyond hope until all your hopes are realised.

This is how what are called the theological virtues, which are the foundation of the spiritual life, are learnt and brought to perfection. Other virtues are learnt at one and the same time without the learner realising it. You see, when you give up time you'd rather spend watching television, or going down to the club, or being in the pub, you are practising the virtue of temperance. And when you continue trying to pray despite temptations and distractions, then you are learning the virtue of fortitude and practising the perseverance without which you will get nowhere in the spiritual life. And so all the other moral virtues, and others too, are learnt just by performing the simple action that is central to all and every type of prayer – the raising of the heart and mind to God.

Secular athletes perfect themselves physically by raising increasingly heavier weights to obtain more strength and greater powers of endurance. Exactly the same happens to these spiritual athletes who are prepared to persevere beyond first beginnings in prayer, as they are asked to travel through 'dark nights' where they face greater temptations and distractions than ever before. These temptations and distractions do not prevent a person from becoming perfect, but rather they are the means by which someone becomes perfect, as they persevere in raising their hearts to God. Gradually their 'spiritual muscles' or virtues are brought to perfection. That's why the more perfect the saint becomes, the greater the 'dark nights' they have to undergo and the greater the temptations and the distractions they have to overcome. If you want to see how the great saints and mystics practised spiritual weight training in prayer, read St John of the Cross and St Teresa of Avila. And if you want to know how this enables God to enter into this prayer until the heart remains continually raised and open to experience all the love he wants to give, then read St Teresa's masterwork, *Interior Castle.* Then you'll understand why she said so emphatically what I'm not ashamed to repeat time after time, namely: 'There's only one way to perfection and that is to pray, and if anyone points in a different direction then they are deceiving you.'

Now perhaps I can return to the subject of the prayer that you have admitted has suddenly become as dark as it was light before. Whether you realise it or not, you too are now being called into the inner purification that is the indispensable preparation for contemplation. I will explain this next time.

Love,
David

43

The Call to Contemplation

Dear Susanna,
Whether you like it or not, you have come to an important crossroads in your spiritual journey. There can be no going back. By this I mean you cannot go back to using the methods of prayer that you found helpful before – but, of course, you've already discovered this for yourself. The reason for this is because you are now being called to contemplation.

Père Lallemont, a famous French Jesuit and mystic, used to say that you could do more in a month with contemplation than in a lifetime without it, so it is important that you journey on as soon as possible into what at first seems a strange new world. This means giving exactly the same time to prayer as before, but now a different form of prayer should be employed. If you go back to my books *The Mystic* and *Inner Life* you will find information on the new forms of prayer that will help you now. Let me explain why you find yourself drawn to contemplation.

For several years, you've been trying to raise your heart to God by using your mind, your imagination and your memory to meditate on the scriptures. This enabled you to come to know Christ more deeply so prayer became progressively easier. At the same time you found that both spiritual and secular poetry moved you deeply, and prayers, hymns and some of the psalms filled you with a spiritual satisfaction that you'd not experienced before. Digesting and assimilating them gradually led you into what has traditionally been called 'acquired contemplation' when all you wanted to do was to set aside all previous forms of prayer and to be still before and simply gaze upon God. After several months of this intoxicating prayer, however, everything suddenly changed overnight, leaving you in a strange and unintelligible world that was not of your choosing, or at least that's how it felt.

However, this 'strange new world' is actually of your choosing. You see you have been choosing to raise your heart to God and you've been doing it for long enough for God to take you seriously. What he has done is to accept what you have been offering and draw your heart, or your will, towards himself as powerfully as you allow him. The result of this is that you feel an ever-deepening yearning for God whilst at the same time you feel unable to pray as you did before.

The reason for this is that in accepting your gift, God has begun to draw your will towards himself in such a way that it can no longer function as it did before. All you experience is a strange and vague sense of longing which pursues you inside and outside of prayer and which you cannot explain to yourself, or anyone else for that matter. Simultaneously you will find that you have lost control over the inner faculties that helped you to pray so well before. Instead of helping you to pray, they now hinder you by generating a thousand and one distractions that pick and paw at your mind from the inside. Added to this, all forms of external religious practice that meant so much to you before mean little to you now.

You may run away if you choose, but you cannot return to the prayer that helped you so much before, nor to the fervour that enabled you to revel in the religious rites and ceremonies that now leave you flat. As I explained before, St John of the Cross said that ninety per cent of people give up prayer at this point, because they don't understand what's happening and there doesn't seem to be anyone else who does.

What is needed now is a good spiritual director who knows by personal experience how to guide you forward, but it seems that there are precious few of them about. There are many who are able to help beginners, mainly because they are beginners themselves, but most of them have little idea of how to help people who are led by God into the contemplative way. Often they assume that the person's inability to pray as they have been taught is due to some sort of spiritual or psychological blockage and make wrong recommendations accordingly, which can do considerable harm to the unwary. I am sorry I don't know anyone near you whom I could recommend as a spiritual director, so I'll have to do the best I can by post.

Love,
David

44

A Ray of Darkness

Dear Susanna,
Believe me, I do realise how hard it is. Let me explain what's going on. The principle I've given you before is this: unlike things cannot be united. The selfish cannot be united to the selfless. The traditional teaching of original sin underlines the fact that we are all flawed, that we are selfish through and through. Nevertheless we are all destined to be united with God, who is the perfect 'Selfless One'. In his 'world', traditionally called heaven, where love reigns supreme, only the selfless can be admitted. That's why the Holy Spirit has been sent to purify us so that we can be admitted into this holy place to experience the fullness of love that we desire more than anything else.

Once the prayer of the beginner manifests the desire for God for long enough to prove sincerity, he begins to direct and draw this desire towards himself. This enables his love to enter more deeply through the Holy Spirit, who is sent to transform us into the image and likeness of the most selfless man ever to have lived. The immediate effect of this action is for the person to experience not his presence but rather the selfishness that prevents it. That's why it's often been called a 'ray of darkness'. The beginning of the mystic way, then, is not full of sweetness and light, but of bitterness and darkness, because we are not yet purified enough to experience his presence, but only the presence of the sinfulness and selfishness that keeps him at bay. That's why so many people give up prayer at this stage, believing that they are on the wrong path. You see, it is precisely because a person keeps relentlessly travelling on in prayer that God can show them their sins far more clearly than they could ever see them for themselves.

Now, at this particular point in your journey, you will not only see your sinfulness as never before, but also at the same time your utter helplessness to do anything about it. The experience is not meant to turn you away from God, but to turn you towards him as the only One who can help you. In this purification, therefore, you begin to experience the need for repentance as never before: that's why it's so important. You'll feel the need to make acts of repentance or contrition for your past over and over again, and to ask for the forgiveness you need so that you can return home to be united with the One who is setting up home within you. However, this purification takes some time – months or even years – depending on your commitment to prayer, before you begin to have a positive experience of the Holy Spirit preparing you to be fitted more perfectly into Christ.

When these experiences first come they not only fill you with awe at the power of God, but leave you in no doubt that the experience of his love comes and goes as he chooses, not as you do. At one moment it is all darkness and at another it is all light, so if you were never in doubt before, you are left in no doubt now that he does everything and you can do nothing but persevere as best you can. He, not you, is the architect of the sanctity for which you are destined. This is why the more the saints experienced the action of God the humbler they became, because no matter what others might say, they knew by their own experience that it is God who does everything. So, in this purification for contemplation and in the contemplation that follows it, it is vital that Christ-like people are formed who will help bring about the 'Christian Renaissance' that will dawn at the beginning of the twenty-first century. This is the only school that can prepare believers for the rebirth of Christ in each of them. Then it will be in and through him, who will come into our world again through them, that this rebirth will take place. These men and women will see the meaning of the gospel as never before, by experiencing it. What was complex before will now seem simple. The 'good news' is simply that Jesus is risen, the Spirit who raised him is now being poured out through him into all who would receive him.

In his first sermon St Peter told us how to respond to this world-shaking news. We must repent to receive the Holy Spirit who will fashion us into his image and likeness. This is not a difficult or complex message, nor is it to be infinitely analysed and reduced to a series of intellectual propositions by Greek intellectualism. It is a message so simple that it is catholic: catholic in the sense that it is for all, not just for every race, but for every intellectual ability, because it's not primarily about understanding with the mind but of experiencing with the whole person the personal love that Christ came to give to all.

Love,
David

45

The Mantra Men

Dear Susanna,
I'm pleased you found what I wrote helpful, but you're not the only one to be confused by the word 'contemplation', especially as you initially received so much help from the Ignation method of prayer. You see, St Ignatius used the word differently from the rest of the Christian tradition. He used it to describe a certain type of meditation when you try to picture scenes in your imagination, particularly gospel scenes. This use of the word is unique to the Ignation tradition. Normally the word 'contemplation' is used to describe the mystical awareness of God's action in a person, working through the Holy Spirit, as they are being gradually transformed into the image and likeness of Christ. It begins not when we choose, but when he chooses. Although we can prepare for it, as you have been doing for some time, it is essentially God's gift.

To begin with, it is often called 'obscure contemplation', or 'the prayer of faith' or a 'ray of darkness', as I described in my last letter. This is because at first the action of the Holy Spirit just highlights all that separates us from the transformation into Christ that he is working to achieve. The 'ray of darkness' suddenly becomes a ray of light when God chooses, giving the believer ever more intense experiences of the presence of God within, as the journey into Christ deepens. Ignatian 'contemplation' is predominantly self-generated, while true mystical contemplation comes later and is a pure gift of God. Although the former can be a useful help to a beginner, once God gives his gift it is of no further help, nor can a person use it again no matter how hard they may try, for reasons I have already explained. This is the point when they need a different spiritual director, because their new predicament is, more often than not, just as much a mystery to their previous director as it is to themselves.

The other use of the word 'contemplation' doesn't come from the Christian tradition at all, but from the East, more particularly from India. Missionaries who have been struck by the similarity between Eastern mysticism and Christian mysticism have imported an Eastern concept of contemplation into our Western tradition. They claim that the two are virtually the same and try to prove it by quoting the 'Desert Fathers', the 'Eastern Hesychasts', the *Cloud of Unknowing* and other Christian mystical writers to make their point. Sadly they do not seem to understand that in the Western tradition the use of what they call a 'mantra' is suggested only after it is evident to a competent spiritual director that God has drawn a person into 'obscure contemplation' and not before. After a short time the mantra has an effect which is exactly the opposite to that which had been promised.

We are Christians, not Buddhists, because we believe in the Incarnation. Authentic Christian prayer begins, therefore, by coming to know and then to love the person of Jesus Christ in whom we find the perfect flesh-and-blood embodiment of the All-Holy God. That's why it begins with meditation. All forms of genuine Christian meditation, from the 'Lectio Divina' to what St Ignatius calls 'contemplation', are directed to this end.

Although the slow, meditative reading of the scriptures is the best of all forms of meditation, any other form that is helpful can be used to suit different inclinations and temperaments. In Christian meditation, a person is something of an outsider looking at Christ, marvelling at what is seen, being inspired by what he says and learning to love him for what he is and what he has done. But when this love reaches its climax God takes the initiative by leading a person into a profound purification, through 'obscure contemplation', so that they can actually enter into Christ in a deeper way than ever before, thus becoming 'insiders'. They may well have felt like bystanders before, but through the action of the Holy Spirit they are in the process of becoming participators, not just in Christ's life, but in his action. It's only when this happens that, in the Christian tradition, a person is taught to use a short sentence like the Jesus prayer, or a brief phrase as Macarius suggests, or a single word as suggested by the author of the *Cloud of Unknowing*. The purpose of this is, in the words of the *Cloud*, to keep our 'naked intent' on God at all times, so that he can enter into us more deeply and bring about the union for which the Holy Spirit has been sent.

Now, what I call the 'mantra men' hand out mantras to all and sundry without determining whether they are ready for them or not. This not only manifests their ignorance of the Christian mystical tradition, but should give a warning to all who are tempted to trust them that they will ultimately lead people astray, not knowingly of course, but through ignorance.

I know you got help from one of these men. Like many others, you happened to hear them speak or listened to one of their tapes at a point in your spiritual life when you needed a short phrase or a single word to help keep your otherwise wandering heart and mind intent on and open to God. This wrongly made you think at the time that they understood you and your spiritual needs, but, as you admitted yourself, you soon found that they didn't. I will talk about this further next time.

Love,
David

46

Pelagian Prayer

Dear Susanna,
You have no need to assure me of the sincerity of the priests who taught you how to use a mantra. I know they are genuine searchers and want to help others, as they feel they have been helped themselves. Their inability to distinguish between Eastern and Western forms of mystical prayer is because, as I've already explained, nobody ever properly taught them their own tradition. Let me explain what I mean.

When people who are beginners in prayer are taught how to use 'mantras' these devices are generally highly successful to begin with. Both the method and the theory are so simple that anyone can follow them and people begin to practise what they call 'contemplative prayer' or 'contemplative meditation' immediately. They have not in fact been taught how to experience true contemplation, which is a gift from God, but a certain peace of mind that can be obtained by the repetition of a mantra. It is a form of mental yoga or self-hypnosis hardly dissimilar to the methods used in transcendental meditation, except that a Christian mantra is used. Similar methods are sometimes employed in the National Health Service to help induce a peaceful state of mind in someone suffering from anxiety or tension. 'Contemplative meditation', 'centring' or whatever else it's called can certainly be very helpful in enabling a person to acquire a certain inner peace, but it is not mystical contemplation. The peace that Jesus promised at the Last Supper is far deeper, far more profound; it is the gift of the Holy Spirit and can never be obtained by man-made methods or techniques.

Having said that, I don't mean to imply that these methods are valueless. They can be useful and can help a person to acquire an inner state of tranquillity in preparation for prayer, but they are not essentially prayer and certainly not contemplation in the Christian sense of the word. However, those who promote this method deceive themselves into believing that it leads to instant contemplation and then they deceive others, albeit with the best will in the world. I have no doubt that they find it helpful to inject a certain peaceful tranquillity and order into their lives, but it will never enable them to lead 'perfect' Christ-like lives. Only the experience of the Holy Spirit working in them through genuine Christian contemplation can do that. However, real harm can be done if it leads beginners away from the Incarnation which is central to our Christian faith. It does this when it leads them away from meditating on the life of Jesus, a meditation that, under the influence of the Holy Spirit, will lead to true Christian contemplation.

This method can also cause considerable harm to those who, after persevering for long enough in meditation, are led into 'obscure contemplation' at the beginning of the mystic way. Finding themselves helpless and utterly unable to control their hearts and minds that endlessly plunge them into distractions, the 'mantra men' seem to offer them the salvation they need. Often they find that the use of a mantra helps, and the assurance that this is the way the Desert Fathers used to pray reassures them.

It is precisely because the use of a mantra provides help that it leads people on more quickly to keep their hearts and minds together and open to the action of the Holy

Spirit. The result is not, however, the peace of mind that the 'mantra men' promised – at least not in the first instance – but inner turmoil. You see, success means that the Holy Spirit is given free rein to begin the purification that must always precede the union for which believers crave. Faced with a disciple for whom the recitation of the mantra has led to the opposite of what had been promised, the guru does not know what has happened or what to do. He begins to think, and perhaps even suggest, that there might be something psychologically wrong, or perhaps some past or present sins that are preventing the tranquillity that the mantras usually lead to. This can have a devastating effect on a person experiencing 'obscure contemplation' because it may confirm their worst fears and set them back by years on the journey that could be facilitated with understanding, compassion and genuine guidance from a competent spiritual director. At this point a person often realises that the guru who first helped them can help them no more and they inevitably part company. However, serious damage is done by someone who, though they may well be wise in the ways of the East, is in effect ignorant of their own tradition.

The form of prayer that such people have encouraged is in effect the prayer of the humanist, and the peace of mind that they promised is the 'apatheia' promised by the Stoics to the person who becomes the architect of their own sanctity. In short, though it has a therapeutic application that can be valuable, from a spiritual point of view it is no more than 'Pelagian prayer' that will not only confuse and mislead a Christian, but can do them irreparable damage.

Yes, I did read that letter in the *Catholic Herald* criticising my approach to prayer. Before commenting on it, let me say that I have never come across Christians drawn into 'The World Community for Christian Meditation Movement' who have not been thoroughly good people. They don't just take the external practice of their faith seriously, but also put aside regular time to go daily into 'the inner room' to pray. I identified so closely with their personal sincerity and the sincerity of their search that I have until now found it difficult to make any criticism of them. Sadly, they have been misled into thinking that methods of Eastern mysticism involving the continual repetition of mantras are not only in conformity with the Christian mystical tradition, but the high point at which Eastern and Western religions meet. However, contemplative prayer is so important for future reform in the Church, as it has been in the past, that it must be protected from any counterfeit.

John Cassian is usually the person quoted to prove that Eastern and Western mysticism are ultimately one and the same. He was a priest born in the fourth century who spent 12 years, mainly in Egypt, studying the teachings of the Desert Fathers. His copious writings had a profound influence, particularly on Irish and Benedictine monasticism. But because a tiny fraction of what he wrote about prayer and the spiritual life could be misinterpreted to appear to advocate the use of mantras, as used in the East, his status has been raised to enhance his authority. This is why my critics have been misled into believing that he is 'St' John Cassian, a title never given to him by the Church. He was explicitly cited for falling into the heresy of semi-Pelagianism. This is a heresy that leads people to believe that they can become the architects of their own perfection, and that contemplation, for instance, can be obtained by man-made means like mantras and other techniques. This is explicitly denied by the authentic Christian mystical tradition. If anyone wants to be guided by this tradition rather than by its counterfeit, then they must look in the first instance to Jesus himself who never taught the use of mantras.

Jesus not only knew that he was filled by the love of God but continually experienced it. It was this experience that was the source of his inner strength that transformed all he said and did. Later mystical writers used the word 'contemplation' in order to describe the psychological experience of feeling the divine life that he felt continually throbbing within him. They taught that this experience could be felt by all Christians who would embrace a prayer life similar to that of Jesus, combined with an ascetical life to purify them from the sins that never sullied him. This is the best possible way to receive, assimilate and digest the same divine life that filled Jesus himself, a life that is continually poured out through the mysteries that he asked us to remember him by at the Last Supper.

St Thomas Aquinas explains this profound teaching in detail. Read what he has to say on prayer, read his clear definition and description of contemplation and his explanations of the ascetical preparations necessary to receive what finally comes as a gratuitous gift of God. No other theologian has been accepted so whole-heartedly by the Church as the voice of orthodoxy. Then read the writings of St Teresa of Avila and St John of the Cross, who were both made doctors of the Church for their unsurpassed exposition of contemplative prayer. Why look elsewhere, trying to find a sentence here or a sentence there in minor or questionable spiritual writers to endorse an alien form of mysticism that has no more than a thin veneer of orthodoxy? If you find the great spiritual masters too daunting, read the works of the great Dominican theologian Garragou-Lagrange. He has written a unique theological synthesis of the teaching of St Thomas, St Teresa and St John of the Cross on prayer and the spiritual life. If you want to understand the tradition from a psychological point of view, read the classic work *The Graces of Interior Prayer* by the Jesuit master Père Poulain.

I consider it my life's work to restate this profound tradition time and time again because it is desperately needed in the Church today. The sad thing is that the 'mantra movement' has been successful because people genuinely searching for a deeper prayer life have found little help from the true tradition and from those who should have been living it and teaching it to them. I have given the reason for this in earlier letters so I won't repeat myself now. Sadly, often when I try to explain what should be common knowledge to any educated Christian who is serious about the spiritual life, they call me an 'elitist' or simply say that they don't know what Torkington is 'torking' about! Yet again, I want to emphasise that Christianity is a mysticism not a moralism. Without the same love that Jesus experienced working in him, we will not be able to do anything, let alone live out the teaching of the gospel: 'without me you have no power to do anything' (John 15:5). If we do not choose to pray as Jesus did, we do not choose to receive what will alone make us into Christ-like people.

Love,
David

47

The Waiting Game

Dear Susanna,
I know it takes the patience of Job to keep to your time of prayer when you're frequently tempted to give it up in order to do what seem to be far more important things for your family. Please believe me, there's nothing more important than learning the patience in prayer through which all the other virtues come.

Only yesterday I was reading St Catherine of Siena. She said that patience isn't so much a virtue as the test of all true virtue. If you haven't got any patience at all, it's ten to one you haven't got any virtues either that are worth writing home about. That brings us all down to size, doesn't it! It made me reflect on why I get so impatient if I have to wait for anything, whether it's for the post to come, a train or plane to arrive, or for my turn at the supermarket checkout. The truth of the matter is I hate waiting for anything, because it means I'm not in control – and who doesn't like being in control, not only of events, but of other people too? In short, we want everyone to be at our 'beck and call', we want everything to revolve around us and to be at our service, when, where and how we choose. To say a person is impatient is just another way of saying that they are arrogant, full of themselves and full of their own importance. Now, arrogance or pride of any sort obscures the fundamental vision that all of us need to have quite clearly in mind – namely, that we are weak and incapable of achieving anything really lasting or worthwhile without God. If we don't see this we are blind and we will stumble around for a lifetime, never turning to prayer to receive from God the love that will alone satisfy us and give us the deep inner security that we need more than anything else. Of course, it's not particularly pleasant to realise that you are several million light years away from sanctity, but at least it's a beginning. But what's to be done about it? That's the important thing.

The answer is to be found in prayer, at least that's what St Catherine said. Now she doesn't just mean praying for patience, though there's no harm in that, but practising patience inside of prayer itself. Most of us give up prayer before we've really started because nothing happens, and we are too impatient to learn to wait on God. All the saints say the same thing – you only really learn patience by practising patience, and prayer is the best place to do it. St Luke is a case in point. What he has to say about prayer is of particular importance because he is handing on the teaching of Jesus himself. He not only tells us how to address God, but what we ought to say to him and what we ought to ask for too. But his most profound teaching on prayer is this: no matter where you begin or how you progress, the time will come when you find you have done all that you can do, and then you have to learn how to wait on God. It is here that a person learns by practical experience that it is not they who are in control, but God. He comes when he chooses not when we choose. Our job is to be ready at all times to receive him.

Waiting on God is easy when he seems to be close at hand, listening to all we have to say and granting any request that we make of him. That's what we call cupboard love, isn't it? But the real test of love is when we are prepared to go on loving, go on giving, go on waiting, when he seems far away, when he doesn't seem to be listening at all or granting what is asked of him. St John of the Cross was made a doctor of the Church because he has written more profoundly than anyone else about that time in prayer when we have to learn to wait on God. He called this important and prolonged period in our prayer life the 'Dark Night of the Soul', and used this phrase as the title of his most famous book. He makes it quite clear that anyone who perseveres in prayer will inevitably come to the place where one has to wait on God amidst dryness, aridity and darkness, where there will be not only many distractions, but temptations too, even temptations against faith, hope and charity. When there's no experience of the presence of God for prolonged periods of time you begin to ask not just where God is, but whether there is a God, and if there is no God, what hope there is. Only the person who is prepared to persevere in this waiting on God despite such temptations will be purified and refined in such a way that they are ready and prepared to receive the One who comes when he is least expected.

This is how saints are made, as they learn to remain patiently waiting on God come what may. It's the only way that we will learn true patience too, by practising patience in adversity as best we can.

Love,
David

48

Endless Ecstasy

Dear Susanna,
Although patience can only be learnt by being patient and that can be a very hard lesson to learn, it is a lesson that can open us to the most powerful experience of God that we can have on earth. You see, practising patience in prayer, as I explained in my last letter, gradually enables the Holy Spirit to purge away the deep selfishness in us that prevents us from experiencing his presence within us.

St Augustine said that this presence surrounds and penetrates us as a sponge is surrounded and penetrated by the water that first gave it life. This is a very profound analogy that helps us picture in our imagination how his love continually possesses every part of us. However, the full truth is even more profound and takes us beyond anything our imagination can picture. We are not sponges, of course, but human beings with minds and hearts. If we freely allow the love that constantly surrounds our physical being to enter our spiritual being, our hearts and minds will be filled too and then surcharged as never before by the divine. Then they will be able to rise with ever-increasing ease to the same God whose love penetrates them. As this love is the same that fills Jesus, it fits our loving into his, so through him we are caught up into the endless vortex of mutual loving that revolves between him and his Father.

To begin with, and usually for a long time at the beginning of contemplation, these sublime truths leave you cold and you feel nothing, but gradually things begin to change. In God's time, not ours, but with our continual perseverance and co-operation, we suddenly experience God's presence within. This usually happens when we least expect it and in a way that leaves us in no doubt that he is doing everything and we are doing no more than waiting for him, as we hold on by the skin of our teeth. Gradually the heart acts like a prism, transmitting the love that is received to the deep inner recesses of our spiritual being and enabling us to experience his action to varying degrees of intensity. Then, in brief moments of God-given grace, we are able to experience something of the 'height and the depths, the length and the breadth of the love of God that surpasses all our understanding' (Ephesians 3:18).

It is in moments such as these that some of the fathers of the Church believed that we could glimpse something of the profound ecstasy that is our ultimate destiny. In these all too brief and fleeting moments it is possible to anticipate the time when we will be taken up out of ourselves and into the Holy Spirit, who is the 'mutual loving' that revolves between Jesus and his Father for ever.

However, one of the great poet-mystics, St Gregory of Nyssa, went further and said that our ultimate destiny is even more exciting, even more exhilarating. In order to express the inexpressible as best he could, he added the Greek prefix 'ep' to the word ecstasy to make the new word 'ep-ecstasy'. The force of this word means that we are called not just to ecstasy, but to continual ecstasy, as we are endlessly transported out of ourselves and into God to eternity. God's love is inexhaustible and so therefore is our journey into it and our experience of it; this is limited only by our capacity to receive, which is itself continually expanded by what, or rather who, it receives.

The beginning of this ongoing and ever-deepening ecstasy is experienced even now in this life for the person who is prepared to journey on in prayer, come what may, far beyond first beginnings. This will not only help us to experience something of the love that Jesus continually experienced whilst on earth, but it will also give us something of the same inner strength that he received too. This will progressively impart the inner power and strength needed to live the sort of exemplary Christ-like lives to which we all aspire, and which is the only ultimate test of any authentic spiritual life. In the words of the gospel, 'it is by their fruits that you will know them' (Matthew 7:20).
Love,
David

49

The Holy Trinity

Dear Susanna,

Yes, you're absolutely right – that's exactly what I mean. We are called to share in the most intimate love that revolves between the Father and the Son to eternity. Frankly, I don't know any fairy story or any man-made myth, no matter how outrageous, that comes anywhere near this mind-boggling truth. Not even arrogant human beings could have imagined it in their wildest dreams, if it hadn't come directly from Jesus himself. However, even he didn't try to define or explain the mystery of the 'Trinity', so how do you expect me to do it? You see, he was more concerned about telling us how to enter into it and experience it than giving the sort of theoretical explanations that would come later.

Now you see what I meant when I said that whether we realise it or not we've all been educated to think like Greeks. That's why you're asking me to define the inner nature of the Trinity, something that is indefinable. You can't define the infinite, because it is utterly beyond the finite – and even if I could, would it really matter? The traditional doctrine of the Trinity that we were brought up on was formulated by the Church not to inspire us but to protect us against the sort of heresy that threatened the early Christians. The truth of the matter is that I've never tried to explain it to anyone, not even to myself. I just use the analogy of human love to give me pointers to what is beyond my comprehension, so you'll have to be satisfied with that.

You may remember that in *Wuthering Heights* Catherine's love for Heathcliff was so great that she said, 'I don't love Heathcliff, I am Heathcliff.' In other words she wanted to enter into him more fully and more completely than their human bodies allowed and remain there forever. She was not so much saying what had happened, but what she desired to happen more than anything else. She wanted to lose herself in him, and wanted him to lose himself in her. You find the same idea in the story of Tristan and Isolde. When the two reached the heights of human love, their union was so sublime that at one moment Tristan actually calls Isolde Tristan, and Isolde calls Tristan Isolde. And exactly the same thing can be found in the gospels: at one moment Jesus calls himself the Son of God, and at another moment, God.

Although the love of Tristan and Isolde is as close as any human mind can imagine, not even Wagner, whose music describes their love more perfectly than any words, suggests that they merge to become a new single identity. Genuine love is between two. And just as there are always two separate persons in human love so there must surely be two separate persons in divine love. Although Jesus insists time and time again that 'the Father and I are one' and that 'the Father is in me and I am in him', it is perfectly evident that their individual identity is never lost no matter how close their union.

The gospels take this one step further. The love that binds Jesus and his Father together is not a blind impersonal force but a separate personal love in its own right. Let me return to the human analogy to try to explain what this means. In *Wuthering Heights* Catherine and Heathcliff see that the mutual love that binds them together seems to have something of an identity of its own that is equal to the love that each has for the other. If anything it is greater, because it appears to have a personality that can unite them, even when they are separated from each other, and even separated by death. In God alone, can the love that may in this life be experienced in some measure as three separate entities, be found in its most complete form and experienced in an endless ecstasy, or what St Gregory of Nyssa called 'ep-ecstasy', to all eternity.

Jesus does not tell us these profound ideas because he wants to exercise our minds with dry abstract thoughts about the inner nature of what was later called the 'Holy Trinity', but because he wants to inspire us with the truth. The truth is that the Father and the Son have chosen to make their home within us, so that the most sublime love affair imaginable takes place within our inmost being. The reason for this is even more incredible. It is for no other reason than that the love that binds the Father to the Son is meant to bind us too so that we can experience it as it penetrates us more and more. The ultimate experience of God on earth, that is known only to those who arrive at what the Greek fathers called 'Theosis' or 'Divinisation' and what St Teresa of Avila called the 'The Mystical Marriage', is Trinitarian. Such people become clearly aware that they are caught up in, and experience in some measure, the love without measure that endlessly revolves between the Father and the Son within their own inner being.

From this you can see that the true repentance that I have spoken about before means nothing other than returning to our true home, which is within us. It is here that we can embrace and be embraced by the fatherly love in whom our wildest hopes and dreams can be fulfilled.

If you read, reread and reflect on all Jesus said and did in St John's account of the Last Supper, these profound truths will come alive in a way that nothing I can say ever

will. Then you'll receive far more than mere words through the Spirit who inspired them, and what you receive will bring you to your knees in adoration and in thanksgiving.
Love,
David

50

Homes for All

Dear Susanna,

Thank you so much for your kind invitation: we are delighted to accept. It's always a joy watching young children opening their presents at Christmas. I love to see them bursting with excitement as they open them, and then playing with them with such enthusiasm that they forget to say 'thank you'. Saying 'thank you' doesn't come naturally to young children; they usually have to be reminded many times over before it becomes a habit. Yet in fact they've already said thanks in the way that really matters. They've shown their appreciation in their eyes and in the way they've shown off their presents to others and played with them with such delight.

It was the same with the first Jews, who didn't even have a formal word for 'thank you' to begin with. If they were given anything they valued they shouted with joy and showed their pleasure at what they'd been given by using it in such a way that their appreciation would be shown far more effectively than by formal thanks.

Almost 25 years ago I spent Christmas with a family who, like you, had four children under ten. However, that Christmas there was a fifth child present whom they'd semi-fostered. She stayed with them for some weekends and most of the school holidays. She was the last in line to receive her Christmas present, which looked rather boring compared with the others. At first the girl looked bewildered and not a little disappointed, until it was explained to her that they were her papers of adoption. From now on she was a full member of the family. She didn't need to go back to the orphanage at the end of the holiday; in fact, she didn't need to go back ever again. Tears of joy rolled down her cheeks, and she ran over to her new mother and hugged and hugged her. Her new father told her they had no choice with their own children, they accepted them just as they came, but she was very special because they had actually chosen her. I don't know if she formally thanked them for what they'd done for her – there was nobody to prompt her – but she more than thanked them that Christmas and for many Christmases to come. She did everything to show how grateful she was for the new home she'd been given and the love that she's never failed to return in kind.

What better gift can anyone receive than a home of their own, a home where there's love that surrounds and supports them, come what may? That's what everyone really wants more than anything else. Moreover, if that home could be guaranteed for ever then that would be the closest thing to heaven on earth. Now that's the gift that was promised by Jesus on the night before he died when he said that he wouldn't leave us as orphans, and if anyone chooses to receive him then 'my father will love him and we shall come to him and make our home within him' (John 14:23).

The more we meditate on what this means, the more we shall be overcome with gratitude and want to express it in formal thanksgiving. That's normal, but the real thanks that God wants is much more than that. He wants us to use the gift we've been given by entering into our new home – 'make your home in me, as I make my home in you' (John 15:4). When this happens we are drawn into the most potent and the most powerful family love ever, a love that endlessly revolves between the Father and the Son. If we do all in our power to become members of this new family then the love we receive will begin to show itself in all that we are and say and do. 'Whosoever remains in me, with me in him bears fruit in plenty' (John 15:5). The first fruits will enable us to do what is asked of us and that is 'to love one another' (John 15:17) – and don't forget that charity begins at home, even if it doesn't end there. This is the only sign that Jesus ever describes of how to be a genuine Christian and it is the best possible way we can thank God for what we've received by sharing it with others. This is far more valuable than an occasional formal 'thank you', though there should be time for that too. When people see what belonging to this new family has made of us, they will want to ask questions and those questions should lead to more and more orphans finding homes. These orphans will be housed in the sort of home that they want more than any other, and in the family that will never let them down, not this side of eternity.

Looking forward to seeing you at Christmas.

Love,
David

51

First Things First

Dear Susanna,
I'm not usually addicted to telling pious stories, but as it's Christmas I'll make an exception! The holiest man I've ever met told it to me in a half-hour's interview at a remote Cistercian monastery in Africa. I learnt more about the spiritual life in that half-hour than in more than half my lifetime.

He told me how he underwent a prolonged desert experience for more than ten years. During this time he had to undergo enormous temptations, the last and most testing of which was against the faith that had so far sustained him no matter how he'd been tested. His spiritual desert came to an end during an illness that confined him to the monastic infirmary for a week. During this time he received a startling spiritual experience that took place in the context of what he could only describe as a weak ecstasy that lasted for the duration. By a weak ecstasy he meant that although he was at all times conscious, his consciousness was filled with a powerful experience of the presence of God that never left him. On three distinct occasions, as he was being given Holy Communion he heard clearly and distinctly these words: 'Only you have been keeping me out.' 'I heard these words,' he insisted, 'as clearly as I have heard yours.' Immediately he knew who was speaking to him and what he meant.

Christmas is a celebration of God choosing not just to

enter into a special human being two thousand years ago but into every human being who freely chooses to receive him. However, the stark truth is that we forget at our peril that we can and regularly do keep him out. My previous letters have given you the wrong impression if you think that there is something automatic about this divine indwelling that Jesus promised would take place in us. If you'd read St John's account of all Jesus said and did at the Last Supper you couldn't have come to that conclusion either. So once again I beg you to read, reread and reflect on the most sublime chapters in the New Testament.

Spiritual writers have always insisted that time should be given daily for what was later called 'an examination of conscience'. Its purpose was to try to find out what we have done or, more important, what we have failed to do to remove every obstacle that would prevent God making his home in us. I say 'more important, what we've failed to do' because I'm merely trying to redress an imbalance that crept into Christian spirituality at the time of the Renaissance. It was then that the new emphasis on human endeavour had such a significant influence on every aspect of human life that it began to infiltrate the spiritual life. This had disastrous consequences by deceiving many believers into thinking that they could obtain perfection for themselves. It was in this context that the traditional 'examination of conscience' was seen as primarily the time when a person had to discover the sins that blighted them and root them out of their lives so that they could attain perfection. It was a spirituality that owed far more to the secular heroes of the Renaissance, Socrates and the Stoics than to Jesus and the disciples who followed him. As I've explained before, the Stoics believed that they could become the architects of their own perfection. Although Christians had been taught that they couldn't, the 'new spirituality' deceived many and pride won them over to a sort of Christian stoicism that's been with us ever since.

It's not ourselves and our miserable sins that should be the first thing to occupy our time, but God and how we've failed to remain open to receive him. Without him we won't even be able to see the real sins that keep him out, never mind receive the power to overcome them. 'Without me you have no power to do anything' (John 15:6). The first thing, then, that we should ask when we examine our consciences is how much quality space and time we have been giving each day to open ourselves to the only love that can change us. Once we get this right then the sins that continually prevent the union that we desire above all else can be destroyed at source. At last the spiritual life will have begun in earnest, because we will be allowing the Spirit in to do in us what we could never do alone. The Spirit will be able to save us from the self-absorption that keeps him out and will show us how to prepare to receive what Jesus promised us at the Last Supper. The sins that really keep him out will be seen with ever greater clarity, whilst at the same time the grace will be given which alone will enable us to overcome them.

A greater-spotted teenage Romeo will never be able to free himself from his self-absorption to become the lover he wants to be until he experiences the love of his Juliet. It is her love that will give him the real desire and the strength to become what he wants to be, and change all in his life that would prevent them coming ever closer together. It's exactly the same in the spiritual life. That's what St Augustine meant when he said, 'Love and do what you will'. In other words, if you really love someone you wouldn't knowingly do anything that could cause them pain.

Once again, I can already hear you saying, 'But where's the time to do this?' I know it's not easy, but let's be honest

– you can find time to do other things that are important. You find time to go to the gym twice a week, to model and paint, and to read far more than I do, so by a little judicious pruning you should be able to find some time for what time was created for in the first place! If you do this, I promise that things will begin to happen in your life that you'd never thought possible before, because at last you've begun to put first things first.

Love,
David

52

Energy Management

Dear Susanna,
Of course I can't help but be impressed by your list of New Year's resolutions. But are you being realistic? I would have thought that giving up smoking would be more than enough to be going on with. May I make a suggestion that will eventually enable you to keep all your resolutions, and even others that you've not yet thought about?

The suggestion is that you make but one resolution that will enable you to receive the strength not just to do the possible but also the impossible. The idea is this: don't give up anything you like or enjoy (except sin, of course) unless it prevents you from giving quality space and time each day to God in prayer. The theory is simple. We're all weak and even if we do manage to keep an odd resolution here and there throughout our lives we will never manage to keep them all, never mind conquer the sins that continually topple us.

Now I know, as you said before, that you have 'to be busy about many things'; who wouldn't, with a husband and four small boys to look after! But for their sake you need more love than you can generate by yourself. So, you see, there's nothing more important than resolving to surcharge your own limited love with love unlimited. This is the resolution to end all resolutions, because at last it will enable you to keep them all and do far more besides. In the words of the gospel, 'First seek God and his kingdom of love and everything else will be given to you' (Matthew 6:33). Prayer is just the traditional word used to describe how we go about doing this. If you make a New Year's resolution to do this above all else and then examine your conscience every day to make sure you are keeping to it, your life and the life of your family will be irrevocably changed for the better. All things are possible with love that are quite impossible without it.

I was talking to Pat about rugby last time we were over and he was saying that now middle age is on the horizon he is finding it more and more difficult to play with anything like the success he used to have. He told me he had to practise what he calls 'energy management'. In other words, he's only got a limited amount of energy these days, so he has to use what energy he has to best advantage. He therefore freewheels whenever he can and uses his energy to maximum effect at crucial moments of the game.

I was just thinking that it's the same with you – or the same with all of us, for that matter, when it comes to the spiritual life. We are all weak and only have a limited amount of energy at our disposal. So instead of dissipating it trying to do everything and ending up doing nothing, we all need to practise 'energy management'. In other words, we need to use what little energy we have to maximum effect. This means trying to organise our daily lives so that we have regular times of access to the most powerful energy available to us. As this supernatural energy or love begins to surcharge our own, we will be capable of doing anything that is quite impossible without it.

Jesus himself did exactly the same because he recognised that in freely choosing to enter into our weak human nature he needed the help and strength that only his Father could give. He realised that he needed to structure his own life in such a way that he could continually have access to the help and strength he needed from his Father.

That's why he regularly went to the temple and to the synagogue with his disciples, and that's why he often went alone for more prolonged personal prayer into lonely places. However, in addition to all this, he needed to give time to daily personal prayer, as we do.

It was the custom of orthodox Jews at that period to pray at prescribed times of the day, just as Muslims do today. Jesus criticised his own contemporaries for the way they made such an exhibition of themselves at these prescribed times, ostentatiously praying in public to impress the 'plebs' with their piety. He didn't criticise them for praying at set times, something he would certainly have done himself, but for the way that they did it. When you pray, he insisted, 'Go to your private room and, when you have shut your door, pray to your Father who is in that secret place and your Father who sees all that is done in secret will reward you' (Matthew 6:6).

Now we need to do the same if we are going to maintain any momentum in our spiritual journey. When life-styles and work-patterns changed in subsequent centuries, Christians no longer found it possible to stick to the prescribed times that Jesus would have used with his disciples, so the practice of morning and evening prayer began to take their place. Sadly, in recent years these practices seem to be disappearing, as does the saying of grace before and after meals – and the meals themselves are too often eaten on a tray in front of the 'telly'.

It's no good saying we simply don't have the time, because it's rarely true. A recent survey for the BBC discovered that an average person watches television for over 30 hours a week. Surely we could give up a couple of hours here and there for the only salt that will give real savour to our lives and meaning to what can so easily be meaningless without it.

I went into our local fruit and veg shop recently to pick

up a lettuce and came out with much more than I bargained for. I made some reference to a television programme that I thought the young woman who served me would most likely have seen the previous evening, only to be told she didn't have a television. It seems that a trip to India with her husband had converted them both to Buddhism. She and her husband spend their evenings reading, meditating and listening to 'contemplative music' and they get up at 5.30 every morning to do the same. Naturally I was very impressed, especially when she told me she'd just returned from a ten-day silent retreat at a Buddhist Centre near Hereford. If only we took the practice of what we believe as seriously as she does! It made me rethink the structures in my own life that had been looking a little wobbly of late, and try to learn something from a woman half my age. Time must be programmed into our daily lives if we are to follow Jesus' example seriously. If he needed daily access to his Father to nurture and sustain his spiritual life, how much more do we. This is the first lesson that all the saints learnt from Jesus, but we get it all mixed up because we read the story of their lives backwards and totally misunderstand the principles of the spiritual life that made them what they finally became.

What I mean is this. We read about their unrelenting selflessness, their heroic virtue and their feats of superhuman asceticism and we wrongly believe that we can only become like them by imitating what they did. This is of course a recipe for disaster that has destroyed the youthful idealism of many a would-be saint. Saints become saints not by performing heroic acts but by first opening themselves, as Jesus did, to the only love that will give them the power to perform these. If we only try to copy what are the effects of love, we are doomed to failure. We must copy the saints by realising as they did how weak they were and unable to do anything by themselves. Then we will open ourselves to receive the love that made them such loving people. In short, they were the first to learn how to practise the 'energy management' that enabled them to manage their lives better than anyone else.

You, like Pat, have got to practise 'energy management' by learning to use what little energy you have to maximum effect. In other words, you must make quality space and time in your daily life to tap into the supreme energy which is love. As this love begins to penetrate and replenish your own, you will be able to attain the sort of heroic virtues that every mother needs. So instead of making long lists of resolutions that you'll never have the energy to keep anyway, just make one that will eventually enable you to keep them all.

Happy New Year!

Love,
David